DATE DUE

'To Deprave and Corrupt . . .'

'TO DEPRAVE AND CORRUPT...'

Original studies
in the
nature and definition
of 'obscenity'

EDITED BY JOHN CHANDOS

Souvenir Press

Contents

Introduction
JOHN CHANDOS
'My Brother's Keeper' · 13

DEAN WILLIAM B. LOCKHART
& ROBERT C. McCLURE
Why Obscene? · 51

LORD BIRKETT
The Changing Law · 71

NORMAN ST JOHN-STEVAS
The Church and Censorship · 89

ERNEST VAN DEN HAAG
Quia Ineptum · 109

MAURICE GIRODIAS
More Heat than Light · 125

WALTER ALLEN
The Writer and the Frontiers
of Tolerance · 139

v

CLAIRE & W. M. S. RUSSELL
The Natural History of Censorship · 153

JOHN CHANDOS
Unicorns at Play · 175

Editor's Note

The decision to commission and publish in collected form the following studies was taken in view of the divergence of standards and inconsistency of judgments displayed whenever, in the course of judicial trial or other public process, the concepts of obscenity and censorship have arisen.

There is no subject, excepting sometimes politics, which attracts such strong, and usually irrational, feelings as the charge of 'obscenity', and, since the outcome directly affects freedom of communication, it is one which cannot fail to have far-reaching and influential consequences.

The contributors have been chosen, not for the opinions they may have been believed to hold, but for their experience of one aspect or another of the cause and effect of censorship.

This book will have succeeded in its aim if only, by its tentative example, it encourages more comprehensive studies of a social conflict, whose complex nature must be understood before it can be resolved.

JOHN CHANDOS

London, 1962

Editor's Acknowledgements

My thanks are due to the Principal Keeper of Printed Books at the British Museum for his courteous help and especially to Dr Eric Dingwell who placed his valuable private records at my disposal.

To Mr C. R. Dawes I must acknowledge a debt of exceptional weight. I had invited Mr Dawes to contribute the final chapter to this book. For reasons of ill-health he was unable to accept, but he offered, if I would agree to write the chapter myself, to give me access to his unique unpublished work *Erotic Literature in England*, and invited me to draw upon it freely and without reserve. This most generous proposal I accepted, with the result that problems of research were greatly simplified. Wherever possible I have gone to the original sources, but occasionally it has been necessary to quote direct from Mr Dawes's transcriptions. For the opinions and judgments expressed in *Unicorns at Play* I alone am responsible.

Finally I should like to endorse Lord Birkett's appreciation of the work of a fellow contributor, Dr Norman St John-Stevas, in his book *Obscenity and the Law*. It has proved of invaluable aid to me, as it must to everyone working in this field.

J. C.

Notes on the Contributors

WILLIAM B. LOCKHART is Dean and Professor of Law and ROBERT C. McCLURE is Professor of Law at the University of Minnesota Law School. In collaboration they have produced the most comprehensive juristic studies of the law concerning obscenity and censorship in America. A list of their relevant publications will be found on page 53.

The RT. HON. LORD BIRKETT, P.C., former Lord Justice of Appeal. Before being raised to the Bench he was, as Norman Birkett, K.C., the outstanding advocate of his generation at the English bar. Literature had always been one of Lord Birkett's special interests and he steered the Obscene Publications Bill (1959) through the House of Lords.

NORMAN ST JOHN-STEVAS. Academic lawyer and journalist. Formerly tutor at Merton College, Oxford and Fellow of Yale Law School in 1957. Author of *Life, Death and the Law* and *Obscenity and the Law*. Legal adviser to the A. P. Herbert Committee which drafted the initial Obscene Publications Bill. Now Political Correspondent to the *Economist*.

ERNEST VAN DEN HAAG. Adjunct Professor of Social Philosophy at the University of New York, and lecturer at the New School of Social Research. Practising psychoanalyst; author of *Education as an Industry*; *The Fabric of Society* (with Ralph Ross); chapters in *Mass Culture* and *Psychoanalysis* and many contributions to international reviews and learned journals.

CLAIRE and W. M. S. RUSSELL are behavioural scientists, interested in the evolution of human behaviour. Their work has ranged from experiments on frogs to psychoanalytical practice; from logical analysis of the methods of animal ethology to behavioural analysis of the plays of Sophocles and Shakespeare. Publications include book reviews, and more than a score of scientific papers, but their work so far is chiefly summed up in their joint book *Human Behaviour: a New Approach*.

MAURICE GIRODIAS, publisher and journalist, is managing director of the Olympia Press. He has encouraged and helped many new writers of merit and has been responsible for the first publication of works by Nabokov, Genet, Durrell and other important breakers of new ground. He also publishes works which would be liable to seizure as obscene in England and the United States. He has long been a consistent advocate of the total abolition of censorship.

WALTER ALLEN, author, literary journalist, broadcaster, formerly literary editor of the *New Statesman*, was a member of the A. P. Herbert Committee and participated in the drafting of the Obscene Publications Bill. At present he is at work on a study of the English and American novel from 1920 onwards, a sequel to his earlier *The English Novel: A Short Critical History*.

JOHN CHANDOS. Author, editor, broadcaster. Director of Productions of Nonesuch Record Series; author *Guide to Seduction: notes towards the appreciation of Eros in the Western tradition*; chapter in *The Police and the Public*; broadcasts and contributions to press and reviews on literary and social history; currently at work on *The Divided Heart*, a study in the dichotomy of the Anglo-Irish tradition.

Introduction

JOHN CHANDOS

'My Brother's Keeper'

ONCE upon a time an international conference was held in Geneva in the interests of the 'Suppression of the Circulation in the Traffic in Obscene Publications', but when the delegates were assembled they discovered that they could not agree on the definition of obscenity. This defect, however, proved no match for their enthusiasm and (as I think Aldous Huxley remarked) 'after they had triumphantly asserted that they did not know what they were talking about, the members of the conference settled down to their discussion'.

The impulse to enforce social conformity is a very old one, immeasurably older in effective expression at least than the impulse of individual man to make a free choice for or against or to amend the current orthodoxy of his time. Intellectual freedom reached a height in the most enlightened days of classical antiquity which man had never seen before, and after the collapse of the *Pax Romana* was not to see again for more than a thousand years. The promethean humanists who, in the fourteenth and fifteenth centuries, broke out of the confines of an obscurantist discipline which had served its purpose, released a torrent of creative energy on which we are still drawing today. Then, for the first time in modern Europe, was heard the concept of man as 'a free agent, gifted with reason which distinguished him alike from brutes and angels, and endowed with the power of growth and development', and out of the concept rose the noble claim for the right of 'free enquiry'.[1] But this new freedom very soon threatened to harden into 'freedom' to worship a different fixed version of truth. The process of men glorifying freedom in theory and forging their own bonds in practice is a dichotomy to be found at the centre of any study of Freedom and Control of Communication.

To start then at the centre, and work outwards: in any superstitious community lurks a mysterious, ambiguous threat, the 'Enemy'. It assumes many shapes. If, for instance, a prosecution is brought today in England or America against a publication which has given offence, the charge is likely to rest on the allegation that the book has a tendency to 'deprave and corrupt'.

[1] Picco della Mirandola *On the Dignity of Man.*

'These are terrible words', as Lord Radcliffe said,[1] and inevitably one asks to what dreadful kind of danger and injury they refer: envy or avarice, hatred or uncharitableness, cruelty or bad faith, or malevolent, hurtful lying. To none of these, it appears, do the words apply. The denunciation 'to deprave and corrupt' is in practice directed exclusively at communications concerning the sexual nature of man, in particular to those which are deemed likely to give pleasure. There is at law today, in the words of Lord Radcliffe, 'a submerged equation of morality and sex.'

It was not always so. When the countries which now form Europe first took shape as Christian states, sex had to yield pride of place in the hierarchy of vice to heresy. In principle the early Church frowned on the whole business of sex, and treated it as one of God's more unfortunate mistakes which had somehow to be lived with until the imminent conclusion of all earthly matters. St Augustine warned the faithful not to have many more children since most of the seats vacated in heaven by the fallen angels were already full.

But the literate class was small and composed mainly of priests. What they might read in pagan documents about sex was undoubtedly sinful and deplorable, but it was not an immediate threat to the very survival of the relatively new order, or to the vested interests with which it was buttressed. Rival interpretation of Christ's meanings and intentions, however, could foreseeably overturn the entire edifice of sacerdotal authority. As early as the fourth century therefore, the Church was far too busy subduing infant reformations to bother seriously about the vicarious sexual gratification of her more sophisticated children. At the first Oecumenical Council of Nicea in 325, not only Arius but his book *Thalia* was condemned. '*Non solum repudianda sed etiam damnanda*', said Pope Innocent I and it was a capital crime to be found so much as harbouring and concealing the book.

In the *Decretum Gelasianum*, the first Roman Index of forbidden books, the kinds of writing which are found condemned besides of course heretical books are apocryphal works, forged acts of martyrs, spurious penitentials and what were deemed 'superstitious writings'. The writers who suffered condemnation by the curia during the next few centuries were speculative thinkers, men of the stamp of Berengarious of Tours, Abelard, John Wyclif and John Hus.

Wisely, from their point of view, the Church by decrees of a succession of synods between the thirteenth and fifteenth centuries forbade

---

[1] *Censors*, The Rede Lecture, 1961, Cambridge University Press.

the translation of the Bible. The theologians of Rome were alive from the first to the dangers of that remarkable book; they already anticipated what is not universally appreciated even today, that by a judicious textual selection of the Bible well-nigh any course of action may be made to appear to enjoy divine approval. Among the prohibitions in the *Index Tridentinius*, generally known as the Index of Pius IV was one against immoral, meaning obscene, books, excepting only the ancient classics, which, however, were not to be used in teaching the young. But this was low in the scale on importance; censorship was mainly *de rebus sacris*. Subsequently, the attitude of Rome was to be modified in some degree in sympathy with the Protestant preoccupation with sex, but the priority of the more serious offences was never disturbed.

As recently as 1897 the *Officiorum ac munerum* taking first things first, prohibited all writing defending duelling, suicide, divorce, or representing as useful any innocuous secret societies, especially Freemasonry. In the realm of sexual relations, so long as the sanctity of marriage was preserved, and submission made to the authority of Rome, the Church, while dutifully thundering prohibitions, accepted 'impurity' in word and act with resignation. The priests of a religion governing by means of the confessional are not likely to become sentimentally unrealistic about human nature.

The pre-eminent seriousness of the offence of heresy in verbal communication was for some time reproduced in Protestant England. Its official voice is heard for the last time in the Licensing Act of 1662 which was aimed at 'heretical, seditious, schismatical or offensive books or pamphlets'. But this was a freak, a short-lived Stuart anachronism which breathed its last by 1695, before the end of the century.

The cycle with which we are here concerned may be taken as beginning in the eighteenth century, and an important early manifestation of its process was the prosecution of Read for printing a work called *The Fifteen Plagues of a Maidenhead*. The case was dismissed by Mr Justice Powell in a judgment of exemplary objectivity. The book was 'bawdy stuff' but, said the judge, ' . . . if there should be no remedy in the spiritual court it does not follow there must be a remedy here. There is no law to punish it.' [1] In their references to the separate functions of secular and ecclesiastical courts Mr Justice Powell and Lord Chief Justice Holt were alluding to an ancient division of authority. In the first decade of Norman sovereignty a number of

[1] Rex *v*. Read (1708) Fort 98.

disputes had occurred between the civil and ecclesiastical courts of law and William I had resolved the matter by removing from secular courts 'cognizance and cause concerning the welfare of souls, *quae ad regimen animarum pertinet*'.[1] William's example was followed by his successors both on the grounds of logic and expediency since it was only over the civil courts that the Crown could exercise direct control; and we find Edward I instructing his judges not to interfere with the Bishop of Norwich in the exercise of his jurisdiction in cases of a purely spiritual nature, *quae mere sunt spiritualia*,[2] spiritual province embracing fornication, adultery and other mortal sins.

After the Reformation the Court of the Star Chamber abrogated to itself the role of court of 'criminal equity', and the right to make punishable offences, acts which were not crimes in common or statutory law. They claimed the elastic and unlimited right to act as guardian of the national morals, *custos morum*, which meant, in effect, the right to punish and prohibit any act which they chose to interpret as 'against the public interest'. After the abolition of the Court of the Star Chamber in 1641, the odium and abhorrence which the name of that agent of crown despotism reaped, discredited it as a source of authority in the eyes of lawyers and laymen alike. But in 1663 after a silly and notorious brawl in Covent Garden the courts had, in fact, resorted to claim '*custos mores*' in order to punish a young man about court called Sir Charles Sedley (sometimes spelt Sidley).[3] In company with two or three other louts of fashion Sedley had caused a drunken disturbance in a house in Kings Street, and hurling bottles charged with his own urine from a balcony on the crowd below, perpetrated a number of other aggressive and objectionable public acts, culminating, it was said, in stripping himself naked and preaching blasphemy.[4]

Here clearly there was a breach of the peace and the offence had nothing to do with written publication. Powell and Holt did not resort to the case when they acquitted Read, and as for the *custos mores* claim, it is one thing to make a claim, quite another to make it good, and the general feeling in the law of the eighteenth century was that it had not been made good. But just short of twenty years later a judgment was passed which was to have far reaching consequences, much further reaching than the court foresaw or intended. A bookseller Curl was

[1] Ordinances Separating the Spiritual and Temporal Court. *Circ.* 1070.

[2] *Writ of Circumspecte Agatis* 1285.

[3] Rex *v.* Sedley (1663) 17 st. Tr. 155 1 Keb 620 Isid 168.

[4] Probably an embellishment of Anthony Wood. *Athenae Oxoniensis* (1813–1820) Vm. IV p. 73.

prosecuted for selling an obscene work, *Venus in the Cloister, or The Nun in Her Smock*. In the resourceful zeal of advocacy the Attorney-General, who prosecuted, claimed that it was an offence at common law if an act tended to corrupt the morals of the King's subjects and was against the King's peace.[1] Accepting this argument, Mr Justice Probyn, speaking for the court said that 'since morality is part of the law of the land as the Christian religion is, an act which is destructive of morality in general, such as an obscene libel ought to be punished in the same way as one against the Christian Religion, such as blasphemous libel'.

With less proficiency in logic than in manipulation of law, the learned judge went on to argue 'As to morality, destroying that is destroying the peace of the government, for the government is no more than the public order which is morality.'

This was a flagrant *circulus in probando*, with a proposition advanced in favour of itself, occurring both as a premise and as the conclusion of one and the same syllogism. But despite the vice of the argument the judgment stood, and in that moment the offence of 'obscene libel' was born, which was destined to exercise the most inhibiting influence upon English literature.

Its full effects were delayed. The eighteenth century still had a future of vigorous manhood before it, but the instrument was forged by means of which the prudery which reached its grotesque apotheosis in the following century would proscribe those who sought to explore the deeper reaches of reality. Mr Justice Fortescue dissented in the judgment, objecting that to make an act indictable there should be 'a breach of the peace or something tending to it of which there was nothing in this case'. The disagreement between the judges was a symbol of the cross currents already in conflict in the life of the eighteenth century.

The bawdy, satirical wit, the frank sensuality, the hearty unashamed appetites, the stately elegance of form in language, architecture and music were all conspicuously and often splendidly in evidence; but this was the world of the 'top people' and their agents, of the nobility and gentry, the clergy and the universities. At the same time, less conspicuously but with growing force, another order was stirring out of the yearnings of transcendental fervour for reform below and salvation above. It was the century of Wilberforce and Wesley as well as Fielding and Sheridan. Within the belly of the eighteenth century,

[1] Rex *v.* Curl (1727) 2 st. 788.

invisible at first but later bulging prominently, the nineteenth century grew to its moment of birth.

The Licensing Act of 1738 castrated the theatre.[1] Writers like Fielding protested and changed to the novel as a medium; sophisticated people mocked at the reforms, but though they did not know it they were already on the retreat. By 1777 *The School for Scandal* was being expurgated, and by 1795 Rowland Hill could write, 'a young fellow clasps a young girl in his arms before all the spectators; what folly to suppose that every impure passion is not immediately excited by such scenes as these.'[2] The eighteenth century was now unmistakably pregnant, carrying a child which would grow up to disavow with scandalised self-righteousness its own mother and most of her works.

The transition from the eighteenth century to the Victorian age is one of the most fascinating and teasing phenomena in modern history, and one which has never been satisfactorily accounted for. The changed appearances, clothes, manners, language, conduct, the relationship of the classes and the sexes were so completely transformed in the matter of a few decades that it was difficult to believe that one era had consecutively followed the other.

In the eighteenth century, during a visit to England, Pollnitz noted 'that amiable freedom which reigns in England gives the people an air of gaiety which is to be met with nowhere else so universally'.

Compare that with Geijer's impressions of London at the beginning of the nineteenth century. He is describing a Sunday promenade in Hyde Park.

'The first sight of this multitude of well dressed and handsome people is dazzling, and the whole would be vivid if the entire mass gave any sign of life other than the movement by which they are borne hither and back again. One scarcely sees a smiling lip, one hears no laughter, one hears not a word. Only the sound of thousands of footsteps and a soft murmur of greetings between the human stream which flows forward and that which flows back. It is a running whisper half an English mile in length and one can swear that ninety-nine out of a hundred of the sounds that they utter are nothing but the words "How-do-you-do".'[3]

We know that the industrial revolution and the expansion of opportunities which it created brought into existence a new and growing

---

[1] At the time for political reasons. But later the same powers were applied to enforce moral prohibition.

[2] *Expostulatory Letter*, London 1795, p. 32.

[3] Both quotations are taken from G. Rattry Taylor. *The Angel Makers*, pp. 31–32.

commercial middle class. The members of this class were very naturally insecure, ambitious and snobbish, and their pretensions are constantly satirised in the pages of *Punch*. In their anxiety to be respectable,
to be 'ladies and gentlemen', they struck exaggerated postures of
propriety, flattered their superiors, bullied their inferiors and set great
store on following a strict code of conduct. In the course of their advancement they had brought with them, usually from humbler
origins an assertive prudishness—part of the paraphernalia of respectability—a worship of industry for its own sake, a suspicion of pleasure
as being a trap of the devil and complete lack of all aesthetic taste or
tradition.

Human nature of course was better and worse, happier or less happy
according to the individual's capacity to adapt to circumstances within
this framework of sententious priggishness and the inevitable hypocrisy it represented, but the framework was unmistakable and the
obligation to conform was only nominally optional. Men could be,
and were, ruined by the social and commercial sanctions exerted by
Methodist and other church groups, and self-appointed moral crusa-
ders, the 'Vice Societies'. Many of these societies' first intentions were
unexceptionable in their benevolence; the poverty and squalor inherited from the eighteenth century had been multiplied round the
'dark satanic mills' and factories where the 'song of the shirt' was be-
gotten, and charity and kindness were dreadfully needed. But it is the
occupational vice of reformers that while striving to abolish one
tyranny they proceed to erect another. The Society for the Abolition
of Vice had a particularly tender concern for the morals of the lower
classes, 'a society for reforming the morals of persons whose incomes
do not exceed £500 per annum', Sydney Smith called it. Gibes like
these, especially when they came from the class whom they particularly
wished to be identified with, filled them with wounded indignation.
'Much prejudice has prevailed against the society', said the secretary
when he appeared before the House of Commons Police Committee in 1817, and he complained of 'public journals throwing ridicule
on the society by exhibiting it as at issue with low and insignificant
individuals such as keepers of green and fruit-stalls, barbers, etc.'

They did not yet fully appreciate, these frowning, bewhiskered prigs,
that they were already winning a long destructive victory. And here is
the hub of the mystery: that they could impose their standards upon
a new aspiring middle class is not more surprising than that a strong
united cell of communists could impose their will on a weak and

divided trade union; but how they succeeded in penetrating and conquering so quickly the sophisticated and seasoned upper-classes and learned professions remains an unsolved mystery.

Part of the highest classes remained aloof and the men behaved in much the same way as their fathers had done, but less openly. The intensely aristocratic Wellington governors viewed with indifference —even amusement—the presence in the school of boys who had carnal knowledge of a girl of fourteen'.[1] Yet little earlier, when Lady Holland had mocked the new prudery of the times—'Hell is never used except in high poetry'—she had been careful to do so discreetly and in private. There must be an answer which a close and detailed examination of every step in the transition may reveal, but it has yet to be undertaken.

Whatever the causes, the effects are indisputable. The spontaneity of the English personality was attacked by a paralysing disease from which it has never since fully recovered. Standards no longer devolved from or through the aristocracy. One of the activities most sternly suspect to the new breed of censors was that of written communication. They developed a veritable obsession with sin, especially sexual sin, and since the only way they could with propriety maintain constant contact with the forbidden pleasure was by censoring its presence in others, they nosed out sex with an industry as indefatigable as it was ingenious. Bowdler, of course, made the early running with his expurgations of Shakespeare's plays and other established classics to make them fit for younger readers. The results are too well known to quote at length:

> Under the Greenwood Tree
> Who loves to lie with me

became

> Under the Greenwood Tree
> Who loves to work with me.

In 1806 John Styles disposed of William Shakespeare in the following terms:

'Barefaced obscenities, low vulgarities and nauseous vice so frequently figure and pollute his pages that we cannot but regret the luckless hour he became a writer for the stage.'

Despite himself Styles writes with an echo of the old vigorous full-blooded world he deplored and of which there was still a residual

---

[1] David Newsome. *Godliness and Good Learning: Four Studies on a Victorian Ideal*. London 1961.

element in himself. Fifty years later his sentiments had prevailed and one can hear at what cost in the flabby style and unctuous decadent rhetoric of Thomas Best bewailing the day that this so-called Christian nation had paid 'almost idolatrous honour to the memory of a man who wrote so much that would not be tolerated in any decent domestic or social circle and whose works, taken as a whole, whatever amount of genius and talent may be manifested in them—whatever literary beauties they may exhibit—notwithstanding the moral sentiments interspersed in them—and however esteemed among men, yet are, I doubt not, an abomination in the sight of God'.[1]

The tone of morose reproach towards Shakespeare's talent and genius is an interesting symptom of that feeling of resentment and disappointed hopes that marked the professional moralists relationship to the artist. The professional moralist, he who is dedicated to the sacred trust regulating the conduct of others, has always regarded the artist with suspicion or open antagonism born of frustration. In the first place he objects to the moral autonomy and independence which the artist exercises in effect, even if he does not overtly claim the right to do so. Then he is frustrated by his inability to harness the artist to his propaganda wagon, or worse, having succeeded in harnessing him finds that the giant's strength, like Samson's in bondage to the Philistines, seems to have evaporated in captivity. Moreover, in the last resort the artist is dangerously unpredictable and should his strength happen to return unexpectedly he might bring the whole temple of manufactured moral ideology toppling down in ruins. In the most puritan and strictly controlled community of ideas in the world today, one man set the moral pillars shuddering as he fell, and the custodians of Soviet morality have been running hither and thither ever since enquiring into the circumstances in which so dangerous a spirit as Pasternak's could have been allowed to grow so great under the vigilant eyes of comrade informers and comrade censors.

The heart of the matter is that the professional moralist seldom has any notion of the nature and alchemy of art; he recognises the *force* of art, and is prepared to licence it so long as it will do what it is told; but he has never understood or forgiven the artist's refusal, or worse, his inability to become a didactic propagator and populariser of a bureaucratic will. The puritan hostility was old when Tyndale, himself more of a poet than he knew, spoke of 'painted poetry, its babbling eloquence' and Stephen Gossen (a failed playwright) declared that all the

---

[1] Sermons of Rev Thomas Best. November 1864.

arts were 'enemies to virtue' for 'he that goeth to sea must smell of the ship'. This hostility to the arts, especially in certain manifestations,[1] descends in a direct line to the period which we have under review and we find sentiments such as 'novels, generally speaking, are instruments of abomination and ruin',[2] not only in the level of the Evangelical magazine but in the exhortations of Mill to Hume when he reproached his correspondent for allowing himself to become 'enslaved to literature'.

This brand of guilt-saturated obsession with sex produced a condition of perpetual and unrelieved inflammation. The thought that others might actually enjoy the exciting sins which they must reprobate was emotionally intolerable. Every situation and circumstance cast shadows which could be seen by those who had a mind to, as menacing priapic shapes, and furnished opportunities to talk or write under the pretext of dutiful correction about the practices which might not otherwise be raised. Popular periodicals teemed with graphic accounts of the manifold improprieties calling for reform. The personal attendance of male hairdressers upon ladies is a fairly typical example.

'It should seem natural for female delicacy to receive as an attendant at the toilet the assistance of a virtuous and well-educated Englishwoman in preference to men unknown, unaccredited and not otherwise recommended than by having been imported from the shores of France or Italy. It should also seem natural for ladies who feel either what is due to their character or to the unprotected of their sex to desire . . . to avoid those (shops) where files of athletic men, ranged in order behind the counter, and employed like Hercules in the service of Omphale in the most minute, trivial, and effeminate occupations of the female sex.'[3]

There is no reason to suppose that ladies' hairdressers of this period were more athletic than their modern successors. The image of 'athletic men' attendant upon their mistresses' or clients' whims made a persistent appeal to the imagination of the period, and may be found, stripped of all moral pretence, in overtly erotic words of the same era.

In the name of modesty, prurience even managed to press into its service the female corpse.

---

[1] St Augustine strongly resented any show of independence in educated enquiring minds, the eggheads of their time, as for example, 'non melius, sicut multi putant, sed, quod est verum, languidius educati . . .' De Opere Monachorum (C.S.E.L.) xxi, 25. And again, 'utinam isti, qui vacere volunt manibus, omnino vacarent et linguis.' Ibid, xxii, 26.

[2] *Evangelical Magazine.* 1793.

[3] Extract from an *Account of the Ladies Society for the Education of the Poor.* 1804.

Every undertaker should employ women for the express purpose of supplying the female dead with those things which are requisite. How shocking is the idea of our persons being exposed, even after death, to the observation of a parcel of undertaker's men.

In the theatre and literature this compulsive pursuit of immorality continued with insatiable and unflagging zest. The Lord Chamberlain's privilege of having first bite at immorality on the stage had taken most of the fun out of this material. When he excised 'She's an angel' on the grounds that this expression was 'impious and shocking' it tended to leave even the most ingeniously prurient mind without straw to make bricks for pelting the tribe of playwrights.

Occasionally, there would still appear a banquet of opportunities, as when Shelley's *The Cenci* was published in 1820—'pollution, impiousness and infamy' in the words of the *Literary Gazette*—or when *The Double Dealer* was revived, in a private performance, of course, at the beginning of the century and the Theatrical Repository exclaimed: 'Down, down with it to the lowest pit of hell, and there let devils act the parts, and devils only be the auditors.'

During the early part of Victoria's reign the censors seemed to have triumphed and the creative writer to have been tamed to submitting to, even converted to accepting, the standards proclaimed by the new order. It was a delusion, the Victorians were preparing a rod in pickle—figuratively and literally—for their own backs. There were a few robust protests from Macaulay in defence of a new publication of some shocking classic writers like 'Wycherley and Congreve', and a more resigned but acute observation from Thackeray who said, 'since the author of *Tom Jones* was buried not a writer of fiction among us has been permitted to depict to his utmost power a MAN. We must drape him and give him a certain conventional simper.'[1]

Victory brings its own frustrations to the censor. For to him a world without obscenity is unthinkable: if obscenity did not exist it would be necessary to invent it at once; and at times the critics were reduced to reproaching a cunning writer like Thackeray for what he did not say, but they were sure would like to have said. 'He never violates a single conventional rule', Bagehot complained, 'but at the same time the shadow of immorality that is not seen is scarcely ever wanting from his delineation of the society that is seen. Everyone may perceive what is passing in his fancy.'[2]

[1] Preface to *Pendennis*. September 1840.
[2] Bagehot, *Literary Studies*, Vol. II. Pp. 187–188.

What Schuecking[1] called the 'moral hypochondria' of the puritan is reduced to its essence in Lady Eastlake's criticism of *Jane Eyre*, in which she says is committed 'the highest moral offence a writer can commit ... that of making an unworthy character interesting in the eyes of the reader'.[2]

This sentiment would strike a chord of perfect sympathy in a modern authoritarian Russian moralist, as would 'the message of the Central Committee of the Communist Party to the Third Congress of Soviet Writers' to Lady Eastlake had she been able to anticipate it. 'Soviet writers must inspire people in their struggle for Communism, must educate them according to communist principles, must develop in them high moral virtues and intransigent reaction of (sic) bourgeois ideology and morals. ... Writers must become passionate propagandists of the seven year plan and bring cheerfulness, vigour and energy into the heart of man.'

With Christianity substituted for Communism and other appropriate adjustments Lady Eastlake would have heartily approved that exposition of the writer's role in society. In Russia those who deviate or rebel are liable to be expelled from the 'Writer's Union,' that is to say silenced; in Victorian England offending writers had their books withdrawn from the circulating libraries. An unofficial and less absolute, but still effective form of censorship.

The meridian of censorship was reached in the sixties and seventies of the century. Having exhausted the possibilities of the lower half of the female body as agents of shame and guilt by placing them beyond the bounds of permitted reference, the busy mind of the censor was driven to move on to the animal and culinary kingdoms, and it became a solecism to ask at table for a leg of chicken, or a slice off a leg of lamb; in both cases the obligatory term was 'arm'. The nursery too was purged of vice, such as the story of Cinderella 'one of the most exceptionable books ever written for children'.

The psychological strain inherent in the maintenance of external attitudes incompatible with internal pressures cannot but organise its own hidden riots of compensation, however crude, perverse or inadequate. Between 1860 and 1880 pornography burgeoned in secret as never before in England. What occurred was more than an increase in quantity, it was a change in quality, comparable to the effect of the invention of the camera in the visual arts, and productive of a representation, which would be inferior to the humane and revelationary

[1] *Die Familie im Puritanismus*, p. 13.   [2] *Quarterly Review* 1848. Vol. LXXXIV.

insight of a creative vision, but productive of a novel, fleeting, cosy impression of present actuality.

In the eighteenth century, even pornography and obscenity had reflected its share of light from the effulgence of classical literature. Now it reappeared mouthing the jingling idioms of refined vulgarity and the clumsy misalliances of formal and colloquial speech that marked the thickening social belt of the literate, aspiring 'ladies and gentlemen'. The movement of expansion was matched in proportion all the way up. There was room at the top; for the top was being enlarged. In the first half of the nineteenth century forty-four earls, fourteen viscounts and eight marquesses were created, more marquesses than had been created in English history up to 1800. The gulf between the artist and the public which was to last a hundred years was now visible in a growing breach of communication and divergence of standards. In the days of Pope and later Goldsmith poets had been distinguished from their readers by their superior ability, not by ideas or language; but the language itself of Keats, Swinburne, at first even of Tennyson, belonged to a private defensive world apart from the general stream of life, and the feeling behind it caused the orthodox critic at best uneasiness, at worst, furious hostility, for the pictures of human relations they depicted when not overtly scandalous, were complex and ambiguous, and therefore a betrayal of the artist's duty to promulgate the authorised version of morality in the permitted pastel shades of bloodless correctitude.

Revolt was stirring in female as well as male breasts; Mrs Gaskell and George Eliot were under acrimonious attack from critics for showing those aspects of life 'better kept from sight', though the attacks upon them were not as virulent as those directed at the work of Meridith, Charles Reade and, of course, Swinburne. The last two in particular did what Thackeray had prudently refrained from doing, raised the standard of open revolt, and publicly mauled their yelping critics. 'There is a kind of hypocrite', wrote Reade in an open letter, 'that has never been effectually exposed, for want of an expressive name. I beg to supply that defect in our language and introduce to mankind the PRURIENT PRUDE.' A characteristic of this being, Reade observed, is itching 'to attract attention by a parade of modesty (which is a mild form of disease) or even by rashly accusing others of immodesty (and this is the noxious form)'.

After being reviled in terms of hysterical abuse in an organised campaign of detractions Swinburne turned upon his enemies in *Notes of Poems and Reviews*, the searing scorn of his offending gifts and independence, asserting that '. . . if literature is not to deal with the full life of man and the whole nature of things let it be cast aside with the rods and tattles of childhood. Whether it affect to teach or amuse is equally trivial and contemptible to us; only less so than the charge of immorality. . . .' He alluded even more significantly than he can have known to that figure of sinister import in years to come 'the eighteen year old girl' and to 'the evidence which every day makes clearer that our time has only room for such as are content to write for children and girls. . . .'

'In due time, perhaps . . . that gigantic *malade imaginaire* called the public may rebel against the weekly draught or daily drug of MM. Purgon and Diafonus. We meanwhile, who profess to deal neither in poison nor in pap may not unwillingly stand aside. Let those read who will and let those who will, abstain from reading. No-one wishes to force men's food down the throats of babes and sucklings.'

But though he might wither the arguments of the 'moral milkmen' Swinburne could not disperse their bigotry. The enlightenment of his proposition was a hundred years in advance of the times; for the next ninety-one years literature in England and for almost as long in America was subject to be a control designed to preserve the innocence or ignorance of a hypothetical adolescent girl, and at times it would seem, a feeble-minded one. In 1868 Sir Charles Cockburn formulated in the Hicklin case a test which was to the great and long disservice of literature. He defined the test of obscenity as 'whether the tendency of the matter charged as obscenity is to deprave and corrupt those whose minds are open to such immoral influences and into whose hands a publication of this sort may fall'.

With the acceptance of Cockburn's test, and its imprecise, undefined and pejorative terms, as good law, the explorer of experience through words was delivered bound into the hands of the most repressive forces of censorship. It would be agreeable to be able to say that the English judiciary in some measure tempered the more ignorant excesses of popular prejudice, but, in fact, the juries and judges vied in a friendly competition of prurient intolerance.

The division between the artist and the rest was complete. If he was tamed into a submissive agent of established forms, he was treated as quaint, comic, eccentric, a licensed fool of water-colours, romantic reveries, velvet jackets and so on; but if his talents were serious and his aim resolute a general alarm was sounded and he was hunted in packs by the censor-proverts who were capable of extracting salaciousness from the incident of a boy carrying a girl who had sprained her ankle. In *Tom Brown at Oxford*, Tom carries a girl who has a broken ankle. 'If this be muscular Christianity,' said one reviewer, 'the less we have of it the better.' The proscribed included Hardy, Meredith, George Moore, Henry James, the unspeakable gang of French writers, Balzac, Flaubert, Maupassant and Co. Such was the state of mental ambivalence compelled that even the brave and dashing Swinburne was capable (in his later years) of justifying the expurgations of Bowdler, 'the man who made it possible to put Shakespeare into the hands of sensitive and imaginative children,' though Swinburne habitually meditated and celebrated in verse the pleasures of sanguinary paederastic flagellation executed upon the persons of just such 'sensitive and imaginative children'.

One of the worst aspects of the law as it stood, and was to continue to stand, was that no provision was made for the consideration of any possible merits a book under review might possess. The judge was the only guide to the literary or other value of the work before the court, and as a whole the learned judges were implacably hostile to learning and the arts and ruled such factors to be irrelevant and the evidence of expert witnesses to be inadmissible. Moreover, there was no obligation upon the court to consider the book 'as a whole' and, of course, it was never encouraged to do so by the prosecution. One paragraph, sentence, even a single word could be wrenched out of its context and gloated over in a court of law as evidence of the obscenity of a whole book.

All censorship is by nature inhibiting to the free exchange of thought, it carries within it the seeds of sexual aberration, and in nineteenth-century England the monster of censorship spread into an ubiquitous sexual perversion operating mainly outside the courts through the public libraries and providing unmistakable sexual gratification to the tribes of censor-perverts.[1]

Bertrand Russell tells of an Anglican Bishop who wrote to him asserting that every word in every book Russell had ever written was inspired by sexual lust. Lord Russell had written nearly sixty books, mostly on philosophy and mathematical logic; he had written one called *Marriage and Morals* concerning sexual ethics, but this was the only one of the books that the Bishop had read, because, said Lord Russell, 'Sex was the only thing that interested him.'[2]

---

[1] Clinically classifiable as *Paraphiliacs*.
[2] 'Speaking Personally.' The Earl Russell. Nonesuch Records. Pye Plus. (Side three.)

Censorship, then, hung oppressively over the mind of the writer, like the dirty fogs that enveloped contemporary London, producing, as Swinburne had said, 'a clipped and forced growth of unhealthy heat an unnatural air.' Being in the last analysis a part magician, the artist was able to work spells of wonderful transmutation, and introduce forbidden demons ingeniously disguised as angels, or at least like Thackeray, effectively to suggest their presence 'off-stage'. But these were tortuous, and above all wasteful shifts. When Hardy was fighting his publishers over the alleged 'immorality' of *Tess of the d'Urbervilles*, he had to compound with his conscience and his needs by expurgating whole chapters and changing others; he even introduced a wheelbarrow at one point so that Clare might carry the dairymaids across a flooded lane without the distressing implication of corporal contiguity between the man and girls. But he made a private resolution to publish the expurgated chapters when he could elsewhere, and finally the complete book in its original form was published in the last decade of the century to loud cries of protest by the censor-perverts. In America one critical lady read it to the end and then, but only then, 'opened the window to let in the fresh air'.[1]

It has been argued that a reasonable solution to the battle of the books would be reached if literature could be protected and plain pornography, or dirt for dirt's sake, be consigned to the flames. To many intelligent people the issue had seemed absurdly simple of settlement. 'The police magistrate's power should be definitely limited to books which are sold as pornography,' said Virginia Woolf. 'Any man or woman of average intelligence and culture knows the difference between the two kinds of book and has no difficulty in distinguishing one from the other.'[2]

Clearly Mrs Woolf thought that she knew pornography when she saw it. So, I think, can I recognise it too, and so do many others. So, for example, did the speaker of the following words:

'I do not believe there was ever collected between the covers of a book so much bestial obscenity as was found in the pages of this book ... there is not a passage in it which contains any literary genius or the expression of any elevated thought.'

Prosecuting counsel was there evaluating *La Terre* by Emile Zola, for uttering an expurgated translation of which a scholarly publisher of the highest personal repute, Henry Vizetelly, was tried and con-

---

[1] Jeannette Gilder in the *New York World*, 8th December 1895.
[2] *The Nineteenth Century and After*. Vol. DCXXVI, April 1929.

victed by a judge and jury. The verdict was enthusiastically welcomed by *The Times*: '. . . it is not always easy to draw the line which separates what is permissible from what is not. But if the line is not to be drawn so as to exclude such translations as *La Terre* and *Pot Bouille* it is plain that it cannot be drawn at all.'[1]

The Times there made a point which it is unlikely she had any intention of making. Vizetelly raised an almost solitary voice in the wilderness. 'It requires no particular foresight to predict that a couple of generations hence—when the tribe of prejudiced scribes who, ignorant for the most part of their own country's literature, now join the hue and cry against Mr Zola—are relegated to their proper obscurity, the works of the author of the Rougon-Macquart family, in spite of their admitted coarseness, will take rank as classics among the productions of the great writers of the past.'[2]

In the same preface Vizetelly wrote, 'Is actual life to be no longer described in fiction simply because the withdrawing of the veil that shrouds it displays a state of things unadapted to the contemplation—not of grown up men and women, but of the "young person of fifteen" who has all the work of Mr Mudie's novelists to feast upon?'

He was anticipating by nearly a century the salvationary adult spirit displayed by Mr Justice Stable when he came to the rescue of the writer in a famous summing-up: 'Are we to take out literary standards as something that is suitable for a fourteen year old schoolgirl?'[3]

But Mr Justice Stable spoke from the judicial bench, Vizetelly stood in the dock. Prophetic social enlightenment is a dangerous gift. A decade later Zola visited London and was lionised by the world of letters. But the man who had championed his work at the risk of his own safety was not among those present to welcome the French novelist. Vizetelly was dead. In 1889 he had been sentenced to three months' imprisonment for his incorrigible loyalty to literature, and the privations of such a short term in a Victorian gaol at the age of sixty-nine broke down his health and he died soon after his release.

One more example should be sufficient to illustrate the extreme improbability of operating in practice a consistent distinction between literature and pornography. 'Who can doubt the obscenity of this book after a reading of the pages referred to which are too indecent to add

---

[1] *The Times*, November 1888.

[2] Preface to compilation made as a protest against the law addressed to the Attorney General quoted by Norman St John-Stevas, *Obscenity and the Law*, pp. 82–83.

[3] Judge summing-up Regina *v*. Martin Secker and Warburg (1954). Published in full in the form of a pamphlet by Secker and Warburg.

as a footnote? Its characterisation as obscene should be quite unanimous by all who read it.'

Such was the opinion of Judge Manton concerning James Joyce's *Ulysses* when he sat on the United States Court of Appeals in August 1934. But far from 'characterisation' being unanimous, there was not even agreement on the bench. Judge Manton's was a dissenting opinion and the day was carried in favour of 'the putrid book', as it was playfully known in the country of its author's birth, Judge Learned Hand expressing the majority view when he said, 'The net effect even of portions most open to attack, such as the closing monologue of the wife of Leopold Bloom is pitiful and tragic rather than lustful . . . the book as a whole is not pornographic. . . .'

The court of appeal was here upholding the important and influential judgment of the trial judge at the prosecution of *Ulysses*, Judge Woolsey, who for the first time effectively rejected the smothering 'Hicklin' test, and substituted as a requirement, balanced consideration of all the factors making up the work, including the spirit and intention of the author's mind and the literary merit of the book.[1] This was an important step forward and an example which was to be followed in England nearly thirty years later through the medium of Parliamentary legislation, in the Obscene Publications Act of 1959.

The American scene is more complex and more confused than the English, owing to the differences in state law and attitudes. Minor officials and some state police bodies worked in close alliance with self-appointed watchdogs of other peoples morals, the successors of the English Vice Societies which, transplanted in America, flourished marvellously and threatened seriously to impede freedom of expression by issuing to booksellers lists of forbidden books. These lists had no official status, but the combined efforts of such pressure groups could often intimidate booksellers into depriving the public of access to works of contemporary and even classical literature, which, if the booksellers had sought redress at law would have been vindicated by the Federal Courts. Litigation, however, is a chancy and expensive pursuit, and not every bookseller had either the resolution or the resources to challenge his persecutors. Authors whose names have figured on such censorship lists have included William Faulkner, James M. Cain, James T. Farrell, W. Somerset Maugham, Ernest Hemingway, Flaubert, de Maupassant, St John Ervine, Bertrand Russell, Upton Sinclair, H. G. Wells. . . . The list of serious writers

[1] U.S. *v.* One book called *Ulysses*. 5F. Supp. 182. (S.D.N.Y.) 1933.

could be continued indefinitely. 'If I feel I wouldn't want my thirteen year old daughter reading it, I decide its illegal,' said John J. Rusinack, the assistant prosecutor of Michigan in 1955, on being asked how he judged a book.[1] The most serious effect of such a school-room regime is the inhibiting, shrinking effect upon the energy and faculties of the creative writer. As Tolstoy said, 'What matters is not what the censor does to what I have written, but to what I might have written.'

Nor were the visual arts always protected any better than books. Said the chairman of the state literature commission in Georgia, 'I don't discriminate between nude women, whether or not they are art. It's all lustful to me.'[2] Then there was a letter written in 1933 by the assistant collector of the Treasury Department which began, 'Sirs, there is being detained . . . packages addressed to you containing obscene photo-books "Ceiling Sistine Chapel".'[3]

These are extreme cases but by no means seriously unrepresentative of standards in local and government departmental quarters. Offsetting this ground-level obstruction, however, was the salvationary influence of the Federal Courts, especially the United States Supreme Court of Appeal which has tended slowly but steadily to move to the defence of at least some literature which had fallen victim to the judgments of lower courts. In so doing they have invoked additional powers by making the test of a book's obscenity a constitutional issue, and thereby assuming the obligation to review independently the lower courts' findings of fact, whereas previously appellate courts had sometimes accepted the findings of obscenity of a lower court as findings of fact, and thus not normally reversible. Mr Justice Frankfurter may well have had in mind the question-begging processes of argument employed about two hundred years ago by Mr Justice Probyn when he made the position clear, '. . . issue of fact is a coat of many colours. It does not cover a conclusion drawn from uncontroverted happenings, when that conclusion incorporates standards of conduct or criteria for judgment which in themselves are decisive of constitutional rights. . . . Especially in cases arising out of the due Process Clause it is important to distinguish between issues of fact that are here foreclosed and issues which though cast in the form of determinations of fact, are the very issues to review which this court sits.'[4]

---

[1] Quoted in the *Detroit News*, 5th May 1955.

[2] Quoted in the working paper of the American Library Association—American Book Publishers Council conference on the Freedom to Read. 23rd April 1953.

[3] See Haight. *Banned Books*, New York (1955), p. 12.

[4] 38 U.S. 49 (1949) 51.

B

Every move to narrow the definition of obscenity was at least an ameliorating factor; and in their sympathy for the needs of the contemporary writer the United States Federal Judiciary were far in advance of the English bench. In England nothing like Judge Woolsey's judgment on *Ulysses* in 1933 was heard until Mr Justice Stable's directions to the jury at the trial of Mr Fredric Warburg exactly twenty years later. It would be agreeable to think that this was because prosecutions against the kind of books which the American Federal Courts might have protected were not brought, but the truth is less comfortable.

The most notorious of numerous attacks on books undertaken in the twenties and thirties, mainly at the instigation of the then Home Secretary, Sir Joynson Hicks, were proceedings against *The Well of Loneliness* by Radclyffe Hall. This was a long, sad, dull book about a sexual relationship between two women. It was generally praised, indeed over-praised, by literary critics, for its sincerity and integrity of treatment of a delicate situation and it would have had no abnormal history if it had not been seized upon by a journalist called James Douglas who needed a new scandal to scratch up for denunciation in his prurient weekly column. His attack on the book was memorable for a remark which must qualify as the most fatuous saying of the decade. 'I would rather', said Douglas, 'put a phial of prussic acid in the hands of a healthy boy or girl than the book in question. . . .' Bernard Shaw offered to produce the phial, the book and the children providing James Douglas guaranteed to administer the prussic acid rather than the book. We have nothing quite in that class in contemporary journalism, though Dr Soper does not fall far short of the standard in a claim he made recently: 'A boy who takes sex because he wants it will tend to take somebody else's goods for precisely the same reason.'[1]

Ordinarily Douglas's windy broadsides might have made no impression, but Joynson Hicks came more than half-way to meet him. Threatened with criminal prosecution the publishers withdrew the book and copies printed abroad were seized on entry into England. A destruction order was sought and obtained by the government, the testimony of expert witnesses being excluded by the magistrate, Sir Chartres Biron, who supported a pronouncement that art could be obscene, by reference to art on erotic statues in a private room in the Naples Museum, with which he appeared to be familiar. On appeal Sir Thomas Inskip, for the Crown, showed just how far the Hicklin test

[1] *Does Pornography Matter?* Ed. C. H. Rolph. Routledge & Kegan Paul, 1961.

could be pushed before a complaisant court when he argued that 'as to ninety-nine hundreths of it (a whole book) may be beyond criticism, yet one passage may make it a work which ought to be destroyed as obscene'. After the verdict there was an upsurge of protest from practically every writer of note in England and letters appeared in the *Daily Telegraph* and *The Guardian* signed variously by T. S. Eliot, Desmond McCarthy, Bernard Shaw, Arnold Bennett, Lytton Strachey and others. In *The Times*, Cyril Asquith (later Lord Justice Asquith), probably the most scholarly and sophisticated mind at the bar, appealed for a change of the law.

But the censor-pervert though challenged was not easily dislodged, and continued to preside in judgment, especially on the lower levels of the judicature where such matters as the life of books were commonly determined. From this time until the outbreak of the second World War books suppressed by court orders included James Hanley's *Boy* and Wallace Smith's *Bessie Cottar*, Huysman's *La Bas*, Pierre Louys's *Les Chansons de Bilitis*, and *Aphrodite, the Satyricon of Petronius, The Greek Anthology* and *Sleeveless Errand* by Norah James. In the course of the proceedings concerning the latter book, Mr Percival Clark, appearing for the Director of Public Prosecutions, gave as an example of 'shocking depravity' the words of one character who said, 'For Christ's sake, give me a drink.'

It seems desirable at this stage to pause and examine at close quarters the process of judicial censorship in operation; and I have chosen for this demonstration the case of *The Sexual Impulse* because this book, being in the nature of an educational work, was entitled to a hearing on its behalf of suitable witnesses. The court was not able wholly to silence voices of prophecy.

At this time, 1935, psychologists and social workers were much concerned over the number of marriages which broke down as a result of sexual incompatibility due to avoidable causes, such as inhibiting shyness and embarrassment, ignorance and fear. *The Sexual Impulse*, by Edward Charles, was an effort to provide a corrective guide to perplexed men and women, written in friendly, untechnical, and sometimes quite lyrical language. It had been approved by Dr Jensen of Westminster Hospital and by Lord Horder, one of the most senior and distinguished physicians in the country. Professor (now Sir Julian) Huxley had written a foreword. The case was heard before Mr Ronald Powell, who had recently made short work of Petronius and the Greek Anthology.

Professor Julian Huxley, cross-examined by Mr E. B. Knight (prosecuting) said he regarded the book as a study for medical students and intelligent members of the public.

> *Knight:* Have not medical students their own books?—Most of the books on this subject are anatomical. There are few books dealing with the sexual impulse.
>
> *The Magistrate:* Do you regard it as a text book?—No, it is a book of reference. It could be used as what is known in academic circles as subsidiary reading.
>
> *The Magistrate:* What contribution does it make to science?—The contribution is in the realm of psychology rather than in the realms of medicine and contraceptives.
>
> *The Magistrate:* Do you consider that it should be put into the hands of anyone?—Anybody of the type to whom the book is addressed.
>
> *The Magistrate:* Anyone who can pay a guinea for it! When you say in your foreword that the book is action-provoking to what actions do you refer—I think that it would cause people to change their attitude to the sexual union—And carry out in the open air what is generally done in private? —Open air does not necessarily mean in public.
>
> *Mr Knight (referring to a passage on coitus):* Is this not dirty?—No, although I am not prepared to agree with the writer it is a view that should be expressed.

Dr Maude Roydon, of Eccleston Square Church, said that once sexual intercourse had ceased to be instinctive as it was among animals, instruction was necessary.

Mrs Janet Chance stated that she was an authoress and social worker, and founder of a sex educational centre. She considered the book served an educational purpose. Her sex education centre was intended for people who wanted elementary help in sexual matters. She had used the book at the centre and it was in the circulating library there.

> *Mr Knight (adverting to a passage on menstruation):* Isn't that dirty and disgusting?—Not if it is spontaneously desired by both parties as the book says. It is purely a matter of taste.
>
> *The Magistrate:* Have you ever given the book to a member of the working classes—Yes. I judge according to the person's state of mind.
>
> *The Magistrate (referring to three verses, two of which were a quotation from Aldous Huxley's Brave New World):* Do you consider this fit and decent for people of the working classes to read?—Yes.
>
> *The Magistrate:* Then I will read them. (*After a pause.*) No, I won't read them. I don't think they are fit to be read.

There was further evidence, including that of Dr Vogue of Edinburgh University, who stated that he thought part of the book dealing with contraception broke new scientific ground.

For all the effect it had the evidence might as well not have been called. Ordering the book to be destroyed, Mr Powell said he thought the book was not 'fit and decent for the people of the working class to read. I have not decided,' he said, 'whether it is of any medical or psychological value. The only thing for me to decide is whether it comes under the heading of an obscene book. It is quite clear in my mind that one chapter is written . . . consciously reckless of desirable convention.'

The tender solicitude shown by the magistrate for the protection of the working classes against threat to their acquiring tastes above their station is a recurrent theme in the mouths of judges and prosecuting counsel. It was last recorded when Mr Griffith-Jones, prosecuting in the *Lady Chatterley* trial, asked the jury if this were a book they would like their 'servants' to read; but the effect of this appeal upon its auditors was such that it is unlikely to see service in the near future.

The appeal was heard by Sir Percival Clark and three lay magistrates. Dr Royden said that *The Sexual Impulse* was a valuable book; she could recommend it to young couples entering matrimony. Suitable books were rare. She could only think of two others.

Mr Fulton (for the Director of Public Prosecutions) urged that the book was of no scientific or educational value but contained the flippant suggestion that fornication should take place in the open air, not to produce better children but *because it was more pleasant*.[1]

Professor Malinowski, the anthropologist, said in evidence that open discussion of problems of sex such as those contained in the book in question was necessary in the interests of marriage and the family of which institutions he approved.

Mr Fulton (cross-examining): Open discussion between schoolboys?—It is better than clandestine discussion.

Professor J. B. S. Haldane said that this book, dealing with coital positions, was valuable because a knowledge of variety was often necessary to avoid pain.

After Professor Flugel had given similar evidence, Mr Seaton Tiedman, a social worker of fifty years experience, gave evidence that 85% of broken marriages foundered on unsuccessful sexual relations.

---

[1] Note: My italics—editor.

Cross-examined the witness stated that it was good for married couples to have knowledge of various positions.

The Chairman: And find out the method which contains most pleasure.

Mr J. D. Cassels, K.C. (later Mr Justice Cassels), representing the publishers, emphasised the scientific nature of the book. There was no word in it not used in decent society. It was entitled to be judged by the standards of today and not by those of fifty years ago. Yet it had been called a dirty book; the publishers had been likened to the wretch who trundelled pornographic postcards and the learned magistrate below had taken chapter seven to mean that there would be indecency on Hampstead Heath! Yet the author was entitled to criticise methods of love-making and had done so in passages of great beauty. . . . Fifty years hence this case would be regarded with scorn.

Chairman (smiling): You must not threaten us with the opinion of posterity, Mr Cassells.

Mr Cassells: But, since your lordship prompted the reference, I will say that fifty years hence this prosecution will be classed with heresy trials and witch hunts. It would be the height of hypocrisy if the Bench, while continuing to punish poor people who were often led into crime by sexual ignorance, banned a book which gave them much needed information.

On 18th December the Chairman announced that the Bench had decided to dismiss the appeal. It was not necessary to discuss in public the reasons that had led them to that decision.

Mr E. M. Forster protested against the destruction of this book at the International Conference of Authors in Paris in June 1935; but this was a case when the pen was not mightier than the sword.

It was a minor mitigating by-product of the evils of war that the stiffly knotted prudery in England and especially in America was somewhat loosened to allow the freer transmission of all kinds of experience. Not that the battle was over or the censor-pervert defeated. In 1949 a violent attack was made upon Norman Mailer's study of American service life *The Naked and the Dead* and it came from an unexpected quarter, *The Sunday Times*, normally a paper inclined to champion literary freedom. This newspaper did, in fact, protest its opposition to censorship in general, but this book, it alleged, was an extreme case of obscenity. All the familiar clichés followed: 'beastliness . . . public interest . . .' and then the inevitable question begging. 'No decent man,' we were told, 'could leave it about the house, or know without shame that his womenfolk were reading it.' This appeal overlooked the relevant consideration that the 'decent man' did not have to buy the book in the first place, or, having bought it, need not leave it exposed to discovery by his wife and daughters if he considered it to be too strong medicine for their stomachs. Alternatively, if he left it out inadvertently the ladies were under no obligation to read the book but were, one would have thought, under some obligation to desist from perusal when the nature of the contents had revealed it as shocking to them as the 'decent man' clearly presumed that they would find it. However, other papers and writers came to the defence of the book and the Attorney-General, Sir Hartley Shawcross, informed the House of Commons that he did not intend to move against the book because, while it contained much that was 'foul, lewd and revolting', he did not consider that its intention was to corrupt or deprave or that it was likely to lead to any result other than disgust at its contents.

But a few years later, in 1954, a series of what seemed likely to have been inspired prosecutions were brought against publishers of high repute over books by distinguished contemporary novelists. These actions had only mixed success and the summing up of Mr Justice Stable at the trial of Mr Fredric Warburg for publishing *The Philanderer* was an evolution of attitude corresponding to Judge Woolsey's amendment of the Hicklin test in the United States in 1933. But the intention behind the attack constituted an unmistakable threat to the writer's freedom to respond honestly to life. For once the writers and critics closed their ranks, summoned their allies and took counsel and acted resolutely; and thus the seeds of the Obscene Publications Bill were planted.

What finally emerged, after much Parliamentary grafting and pruning was not of the strength and proportions envisaged by the originators of the scheme, but in terms of Parliamentary compromise it may be deemed a qualified success. At long last expert evidence was formally admissible, regarding the literary, scientific or other significant merits of a work; the author's intentions and the kind of public aimed at by the publishers became a relevant consideration. In short, a work under scrutiny of the court was to be judged by its general character and dominant effect.

By an act of legislature the English government had brought its intentions into parallel with those expressed in the attitude of the United States Supreme Court of Appeal. These intentions were to protect the freedom of literature while leaving the police unimpaired authority to act against 'pornography'.

This proposition pleased nearly everybody, dispensing a warm glow of judicious cultural enlightenment, while placating that most interestingly persistent 'hard core' compulsion to blot out 'hard-core' pornography.

We shall presently consider why pornography should draw upon itself such unquestioning, self-righteous intolerance. Meanwhile it is timely to note that the first prosecution in England under the Obscene Publications Act was brought against just the kind of book that the Act had been devised to protect from prosecution. Whatever one may think of the merits of D. H. Lawrence, he was a serious writer whose influence upon modern literature has been substantial. The importance to freedom of communication of the acquittal of Penguin Books has been perhaps exaggerated by the jubilant partisans of literature. It has yet to be seen how the Act will work when applied to less powerfully armed and financed, though not necessarily less deserving, cases. Ironically, Lawrence, himself not in the least a tolerant man about anything, and very cocksure about everything, also thought, like so many others, that he could easily recognise genuine pornography, which he would have censored 'rigorously'. But it was as the most horrible indefensible pornography—'evil outpourings, sewers of French Pornography'—that his book was attacked. That of course was in 1929.

May it then be said at least that today his controversial book has at last been acquitted of these charges in the judgment of all reasonably educated students of modern literature? No, not even as much as that may be said with accuracy. The author of *Lolita* has never been accused of prudery or lack of literary sophistication, but Vladimir Nabokov recently expressed the view that *Lady Chatterley's Lover* was not only a dull book but *pornographic*. It will be remembered that 'obscene and pornographic' were what *Lolita* was described as being when this book first appeared in England and pressure was brought from certain quarters to inspire a prosecution of its publishers, unsuccessfully, on this occasion, as it turned out, but only by a narrow margin.

In a valiant effort to contain the uncontainable, American jurists have lately invoked the service of a concept which they call 'variable obscenity', which briefly postulates that what may be obscene in one context of time and place may not necessarily be obscene in another. This little charmer, of whom much is expected, could prove a siren that would lure the judiciary into deep and treacherous currents. The following short glissade will suggest the kind of oceanic mutations which could lie ahead.

'Is "the average person" always the proper hypothetical person to whose prurient interest the material must appeal? What of material, prurient to the average person, addressed to an audience of persons to whom the material has no prurient appeal? Or of material without prurient appeal to the average person addressed to an audience to whom it has a high degree of prurient appeal?'[1]

The learned commentators who wrote that paragraph were merely paddling in the shallows of the possibilities suggested by variable obscenity.[2]

There is no doubt that English courts and even more so the American have been alive to the duty to protect the writer from the worst excesses of ignorant and irrational prejudice. The necessity of Mr Justice Brandeis's 'clear and present danger' has been applied as a brake: but while the phrase sounds comforting, it is of course too imprecise to affect anybody's judgment. 'Clear and present danger' is where you find it and a Comstock finds it everywhere.

In 1959 the Supreme Court of Appeal reversed the New York Court of Appeals' decision prohibiting the showing of a film of *Lady Chatterley's Lover*. The grounds of the reversal were that the City of New York Statute invoked by the lower court was unconstitutional inasmuch as it violated the freedom of expression guaranteed under the First Amendment.[3] The immediate result was a spate of attacks upon the Supreme Court from sources both inside and outside Congress which all seemed to enjoy in common one advantage over the Supreme Court, perfect and immediate intelligence regarding laws of God and Man. Senator Herman E. Talmadge referred to the 'shocking' decision of the Supreme Court in the following terms: 'By that edict, that court, which had already set itself above the laws of man, undertook also to set itself above the laws of God.' Having observed that 'the Supreme Court is notorious for its ultraliberal rulings,' he issued this warning: 'But, one or two more like this latest in the ultra for freedom and only Congress can save us. If Congress can't then there must be an amendment to the constitution. We must save ourselves.'[4] The *American*

[1] Lockhart and McClure. *Censorship of Obscenity*, Minnesota Law Review, Vol. 45: 5. p. 49.

[2] The U.S. Supreme Court of Appeal is believed in some quarters to be flirting with the idea of 'variable obscenity' but as yet no official engagement has been announced.

[3] Kingsley Int'l Pictures Corp. *v.* Regents of the Univ. of New York. 360 U.S. (1959).

[4] See Lockhart and McClure. *Censorship of Obscenity*, Minnesota Law Review, Vol. 45: 5, 1960, p. 43, footnote 226.

Mercury published articles claiming in terms depressingly familiar to those of us who were adult Europeans before the war, that the interpretation of Constitutional law was the result of a gigantic conspiracy, 'anti-Christian, Jewish and communist inspired.'[1]

Outbursts of intolerance like these may be considered inevitable in a young, highly complex and ambitious society, which is trying to direct and unify an enormous intake of diverse and often incongruous and conflicting racial elements of temperament, character and moral and religious habits. But the standards animating these protests against freedom of thought may have been seen in militant parade a hundred years previously in England. It was in Victorian England that the neo-barbaric heresy was first propounded, boldly and unequivocally as a 'way of life'. Previously there had always been successive reforming spirits correcting this and that, frowning upon the disinterested dedication of philosophers and artists and telling them what they ought to be doing, but it was in Victorian England, for the first time, that the image of the Philistine, pious, industrious, energetic—but still Philistine, to whom the arts were frivolous inessentials—was set up as an *ideal*. In the degeneration of the heroic Philistine into the Plain Man we have seen the consequences as clearly as they can be seen in thought, word and action of aesthetic malnutrition.

The words of Gilbert Armitage come to mind. 'Disdain is too delicate a weapon to penetrate the scale-armoured complacency of so monstrous a pachyderm as a just literate mass democracy of contemporary dimensions. The isolated few who still conserve some respect for the integrity of the intellect and who can still take some pleasure in the things of the mind, must therefore, put off their resignation, overcome their distaste, disregard the possibility of appearing both boring and obvious, and fight for the very existence of the values they care for, by laboriously analysing, explicating and exploding the vast complexes of ignorant prejudice that loom and threaten in every quarter.'[2]

Those words were written in 1935: they remain seriously, though subject to relapses, less critically relevant today.

A flight of questions which has been hovering impatiently over the progress of this tour of inspection now insist on being heard. 'Why have book censorship at all? It only seems to create endless complica-

---

[1] Benedict: 'The *Lady Chatterley's Lover* Case', *American Mercury*, Jan. 1960, p. 3; and 'Pornography, a Political Weapon', *American Mercury*, Feb. 1960, p. 3.

[2] Gilbert Armitage. *Banned Books* (1932).

tions and insoluble problems of interpretation. Why not let everyone write what he wishes?'

To this proposition there is immediate and emphatic objection from several quarters. The first and most sweeping claim for censorship suggests that there 'is then a danger that literature challenging or questioning accepted moral standards of the community might actually bring about a change in the commonly accepted standards?'[1]

It certainly might, for that is what literature and all forms of communication do, and are meant to do. The morals of society are modified and amended by argument, illustration and disputation as well as by example. To try to frustrate such communications would be to violate the principle of freedom of expression on matters of public interest. Without changes in morality we should still have the rack, trials for witchcraft, child labour in mines, slavery, proscription of contraceptives, with its corollary—the tyranny of childbirth. The main issues between political parties are reducible to moral differences.

Disregarding then, such obsolete arguments which consistent judicial repudiation has already disarmed, we are left with one 'hardcore' residual case for censorship, which in essence amounts to this: 'We must have censorship to suppress rank obscenity, pornography.' When the word obscenity comes in (unchaperoned) at the door, reason tends to go out of the window. The chorus of objections in the air includes the voices of the majority of the liberal lawyers who have made important contributions to the battle against the mind of the censor-pervert. Mr Justice Stable, for instance, in the summing up which contained such a persuasive plea for the rights of literature also alluded to 'the filthy, bawdy muck that is just filth for filth's sake ought to be stamped out and suppressed'. Even the American jurists Lockhart and McClure, who are perhaps the coolest and most objective commentators of the laws governing obscenity, would retain censorship because 'hard core pornography is so foul and so revolting that few people can contemplate the absence of laws against it—that would be unthinkable'.[2] Rejecting any ribald suspicion of a disposition by professionals to keep the game alive, one cannot but note with interest that in their predicament, even seasoned lawyers jettison their prudent, measured terms and resort to the war dance and scurrilous epithets of emotional anathema, 'Vile, sewers, exploit dirt for dirt's sake, pander, pollution':, and so on.

[1] See Chafee. *Government and Mass Communication*, pp. 197, 211.
[2] *Censorship and Pornography*. Minnesota Law Review, Vol. 45: 5 (1960) p. 26.

The words scream from judicial reports like an operatic top C in the middle of a discreetly intoned litany. The most candid judges had confessed they found it impossible to be rational about obscenity and Sir Patrick Devlin has shown a disquieting readiness to assent to its withdrawal from the realm of rational consideration altogether, delivering the question of obscenity and indeed morals to the judgment of a 'reasonable man', who is not, it must be noted, required to reason, his right to the dignity of this description resting entirely on absence of any distinction save that of being summoned to serve as a juryman.[1]

But the nature of the offence of obscenity is the very core of the matter and so, isolating obscenity from all protective claims to justification as a legitimate element in Literature, Art and like majesties, we must ask on what grounds does the case rest for depriving it of the constitutional protection of freedom of expression.

The conventional answer to this is in two parts: first, that obscenity is offensive to a significantly large proportion of the community and to their standards, and that in any case, the suppression of obscenity is a matter of no consequence since, in the words of Mr Justice Brennan, it is 'utterly without redeeming social importance'.[2] But these two arguments neutralise each other in mutual contradiction. Obscenity cannot be simultaneously 'unimportant' and important enough by reason of the offence it gives to warrant its exclusion from the constitutional protection to the right of free expression.

If the principle of freedom of expression is to command respect it must mean expression of matter with which some of us may strongly disapprove, not simply of matter with which we all agree or deem innocuous; that would be an empty sham of freedom. What then is 'obscenity'? Taking it to mean what is repulsive, indecent in the affront it offers to one's own standards, then I see obscenity all around me every day, in newspapers, on advertisements, on the television. But what is obscene to one person may not be obscene to another. George Orwell had to study the prayer book for some days before his wedding to steel himself, he said, 'against the obscenities of the wedding service'. And steel himself he did. I find the attitude towards sex of an English Evangelist called Soper 'obscene', but I would not wish to prevent his expressing his views, any more than I would wish to

---

[1] Sir Patrick Devlin. *The Enforcement of Morals.* Maccabean Lecture in Jurisprudence. 1959.

[2] Roth *v.* U.S. 345 U.S. 484 (1957).

prevent a man smoking a pipe of (to me) revolting tobacco, providing he abstained from this practice in enclosed places of public congress, although there is medical evidence that persistence in this habit of smoking may be physically harmful to him. This brings us to the second part of the case for excluding obscene publications from protection: that obscene writing—pornography—is harmful, is liable to 'deprave and corrupt'. For a long time after Cockburn's 'Hicklin test' there was no clear exposition of what was meant by these words. Fulminations from the bench were more invective than argument; one gathered inferentially that it had something to do with sex and a girl whose age fluctuated between fifteen and nineteen and for whose welfare bewigged gentlemen palpitated tenderly when they saved her from the fate worse than death of exposure to the allurement of a work like James Joyce's *Ulysses*. 'Alluring', it will be found, is a key word to the puzzle and a clearer meaning of the court's intention was finally distilled as 'tending to stir sexual impulses and to lead to impure and lustful thoughts,' and by implication, 'actions!' Leaving aside the ambiguous and undefined 'impure', for what is pure to one person may be impure to another, we may note in passing that in practice 'impure' both in England and America appears to mean what is enjoyed! The critical, the unforgivable offence is to give pleasure. In Judge Woolsey's judgment on *Ulysses*, a most liberal process in its time, he justifies the dissemination of Joyce's book because whereas 'in many places the effect of *Ulysses* upon the reader undoubtedly is somewhat emetic, nowhere does it tend to be aphrodisiac'. *Ulysses* may therefore be admitted to the United States.[1] Sir Hartley Shawcross applied a similar protective test when he decided to tolerate *The Naked and the Dead* because he did not think that it was likely to lead to any other result than 'disgust'.

In England and America, it appears one vindicates a book by its capacity to induce vomiting. We are now down to the rock bottom of the whole subject's foundations with the pair of questions, 'What libidinous thought is a book forbidden to excite, and why? What evidence is there that such books do have this influence upon the young whom the courts are concerned to protect, to an extent sufficient to justify the withdrawal of constitutional protection from one class of publication?' First, libidinous thoughts: the most common ones, heterosexual thoughts. It is not an offence in England or America to entertain thoughts of a heterosexual nature, it will be an ominous day

[1] U.S. *v.* One Book called *Ulysses*. 5F. Supp. 182 (S.D.N.Y.) (1933).

when it is. It is not an offence to engage in heterosexual intimacy. If there is a valid argument why it is unlawful to publish matter which may influence people to commit an act which is not in itself unlawful, I have yet to hear it.

The sinister effects of pornography upon susceptible minds have been offered persistently in didactic pronouncements from the bench to justify the imposition of restriction upon freedom of expression. It is intriguing to speculate on the routes by which judges reached this conclusion because no clear indication of the effects of pornography exists. Almost no organised scientific study of the effect has been undertaken: virtually none in England. A little as a by-product of other studies in America is all we have to go on, and such evidence as does exist suggests that the influence of books upon the sexual life of the young is much less than has been enthusiastically supposed in certain vocal quarters.

From what little is known the following is a fair sample of the evidence. Out of 13,528 boys interviewed in an enquiry conducted by the New York City Bureau of Social Hygiene only 4% named books as the source of their sex information. Out of 409 responses from women graduates to the question what did they find most sexually stimulating, 95 said books, 208 said Man. Information from other sources demotes books from their imagined eminence in the scale of influences over people to a point below many other sexual stimulants, music, dancing, all kinds of scents and perfumes, clothes, etc.

The juvenile delinquent, concern for whom animates the loudest demands for censorship, seems in fact almost uninfluenced by books. Sheldon and Eleanor Glueck, who have made an exhaustive study of the factors and influences which might lead to or explain juvenile delinquency, recently published the result of ten years work, in which they catalogued and analysed ninety contributory influences towards delinquency: books were not among them.[1] Other studies confirm the insignificance of reading as an aphrodisiac to the young.[2]

We are now left with the fairly reasonable suspicion that the extremities of inflamed anxiety over the corruption of youth may be themselves a form of veiled obscenity, the fantasies of the censor-pervert,

[1] Glueck. *Unravelling Juvenile Delinquency*, pp. 160–161. (1950).

[2] See Alpert. *Judical Censorship of Obscene Literature*, 52 Harv. C. Rev. 40, 74 (1938). Ernest and Lindey: *The Censor Marches On*, p. 255 (1940). Scott: *Into Whose Hands*, p. 204. (1945). Also see Lockhart and McClure: *Literature, the Law of Obscenity and the Constitution*. Minnesota Law Review, Vol. 38: 4, March 1954.

who needs to disguise the nature of the intensity of his reactions to pornography.

Much pornography is not erotic in any degree except to the particular fantasy to which it caters, and is indeed to most of us simply repellently obscene. As far as I have been able to judge on what evidence exists, pornography is the expression of the effects of influences and experiences other than reading upon the reader and usually the writer, and not itself a direct cause of these effects. Pornography is important for two reasons: first, its alleged dangers have been urged as a justification for curtailment of a very important basic freedom: and second, a society which does not understand its erotic writing does not understand itself. If one is to make a serious attempt to understand it, certain facts which are habitually run away from must be faced and engaged. Demand for pornography does not come from an insignificant fringe of immature youth and sexual invalids. The market for it comes mainly from people of superior education and attainments frequently of public distinction. We must almost certainly reconcile ourselves to some degree of pornography. In a complex society where so much experience is entirely vicarious it would be unnatural if some sexual tastes were not of a complex and vicarious nature. In order to contain and temper these tastes it is necessary that their causes shall be investigated and studied. Such evidence as has been available to me suggests that the causes will be found outside pornography itself, which is simply the servant of tastes which have been established previously by other means. Pornography flourishes and literature withers under censorship: for pornography, whether repellent or alluring, is repetitive and monotonous and by its very nature unsatisfying, so that it profits from prohibition and the consequent circumstances of stimulating secrecy, and rationed dispensation in small doses. If my own experience can produce any original contribution to the subject it may be this: a likely cure of any curiosity about pornography would be an enforced course of reading of obscenity, supplemented by the obligation to make a detailed report on the material.

The domain of private morality is a very important one in society, but it is not a fit subject for legislative control. Such interference would be a violation of the freedom of choice which is one of the ends which our society is pledged to protect: and its only effect would be to bring the law into contempt as past attempts to put Dionysius to death have always done.

We have been a long time struggling towards freedom of the mind.

In 1797 Mr Justice Ashurst said of blasphemy that it was 'not only an offence against God, but against all laws and government from its tendency to dissolve all bonds and obligations of society'.[1]

By 1908 Mr Justice Phillimore was able to say: 'A man is free to think, to speak and to teach what he pleases as to religious matters, but not as to morals.'[2]

In 1959 a judge—an American judge of the Supreme Court of Appeal—actually said in the course of judgment, that judges possessed 'no special expertise to supervise the private morals of the nation'.[3]

The speaker, Mr Justice Black, stands in the extreme vanguard of a Jeffersonian tradition which has previously enjoyed more honour than authority in the superior courts of the United States. But not far behind him in support is Mr Justice Douglas and there are others who sometimes face in the same direction. The situation encourages hope, not complacency. Intolerance, like the will to war, can surge up without obvious warning, a virulent contagion that attacks and destroys indiscriminately the noble and the vulgar. In Athens Socrates lived and taught without serious hindrance until he was seventy. Then one day the old man was framed and condemned. His crime? It should not be difficult to guess if one did not know—corrupting the young. He whom his enemies would destroy they first accuse of immorality.

A parting illustration of ever-present danger. Since a decision in the House of Lords in May 1961[4] it has been shown to be possible for a man to be convicted and punished for an act which was not known to be a breach of law when he committed it. In view of the enthusiasm with which the prosecution appears to have been conducted it will not come as a surprise that there was a sexual element in the offence.

A man had sought to facilitate communication between whores and their clients by publishing a journal called *The Ladies' Directory*, which provided subscribers with particulars of the addresses, physique, hours of business and other intelligence concerning these ladies and their special skills. He was charged with and convicted of three offences: publishing obscene matter, living on the immoral earnings of prostitution, and *conspiring to corrupt public morals*. The production of the latter charge caused surprise and concern in juristical circles where it had been supposed to have been long out of commission along with the pillory, branding, judicial mutilation, and other relics of more despotic times.

---

[1] Rex *v.* Williams 26 st. to 653, at 715.   [2] Rex *v.* Boulter 72. J.P. p. 88.

[3] Kingsley Int'l Pictures Corp. *v.* Regents of the Univ. of N.Y. 360 U.S. 684, 690 (1959).

[4] Shaw *v.* Director of Public Prosecutions (1961) 2 W.L.R. 897.

The charge of conspiracy to corrupt public morals is a relic of the infamous Court of the Star Chamber, an instrument of 'arbitrary and uncertain form of government' which since the eighteenth century had fallen into desuetude in favour of what James Harington in 1656 first called, 'government of laws and not of men'. Now, by a majority decision of the House of Lords to dismiss the appeal against the 'conspiracy' conviction, these virtually limitless powers are revived. Lord Simonds, speaking for the majority (Lord Reid notably dissenting) was careful to repudiate any claim for the courts to legislative power, but legislative power, whatever the noble lord may have purported, is in effect, what this decision has bestowed upon the courts—and retrospective power at that—nothing less than the power to create and punish offences which were not offences at the time of their commission. By this process a man may now be convicted and sentenced for an action which was not known to be a crime when he did it. The limitations which the law of England had carefully built round particular offences are over-run by a general licence to decree'—wide discretionary powers', as Lord Simonds called it—and the interpretation of the intentions of society, historically one of the gravest responsibilities of Parliament, becomes liable to be turned over to an untrained, ephemeral group of jurymen, picked at random, and entrusted with the resolution of such ambiguous and far-reaching issues as 'conspiracy to corrupt public morals' without their having any clear directive of the kind of morality referred to. The even looser notion of 'public mischief' is also being given a new lease of life by Lord Simonds's judgment, and could be extended indefinitely, far beyond the field of sexual morals. Is not this 'government of men' in the worst sense of the word? for it delivers us into the power of a court, which, when it chooses may be a 'lawless' court, in the meaning of law as 'known rules'.

The moral, to one layman at least, is plain and clear. Neutrality is too costly an indulgence by far when freedom of expression is involved. For, of all the advances of civilisation during the past five hundred years, the right to freedom of thought and communication is to me the most precious. It is also, as I have tried to show, the most vulnerable to the hostilities of irrational superstition. Philosophical argument, scientific investigation, historical criticism, psychological revelation have been at different times 'treason', 'heresy', 'blasphemy', 'obscenity'. Accordingly, for my part, I feel obliged to treat freedom to communicate as indivisible, and to defend the right of my neighbours to write and read what they choose, whether it be what I agree with or respect, or what I deem insignificant, fallacious or detestable. And if pornography happens to be what they choose to read, then I will defend their right to read pornography, be their names de Musset, Swinburne and Mark Twain, or just Smith, Jones and Brown.

WILLIAM B. LOCKHART
AND
ROBERT C. McCLURE

Why Obscene?

IN many areas of law there is great confusion about both ends and means. In these areas we know little or nothing of the ends we hope to achieve or of the effectiveness of the means adopted to reach whatever ends we may vaguely feel ought to be achieved. And in most instances the confusion may be attributed to intuitive or common-sense ethics of conscience—a very simple and atomistic system of ethics that lacks rational and systematic development and ignores as irrelevant the contributions that positive social science can make in the clarification of the ends we seek and the means we adopt to achieve them.

No area of law better illustrates this confusion than the law governing the censorship of obscenity. For in this area of law we either do not know or cannot agree upon what is obscene, why we want to censor whatever some or many of us may regard as obscene, or the effects of the censorship means we have adopted to censor obscenity. We are—all of us—still in the blissfully ignorant position of the delegates to the old Geneva Conference on the Suppression of the Circulation and Traffic in Obscene Publications, who discovered that they could not define obscenity, and then 'having triumphantly asserted that they did not know what they were talking about . . . settled down to their discussion'.

In the United States, as in England, the modern confusion in the law of obscenity began with the celebrated Hicklin case of 1868, a case that arose out of the seizure of a pamphlet entitled *The Confessional Unmasked* which had been published by the Protestant Electoral Union as a part of its programme to advance Protestantism and oppose Catholicism, particularly in the election of Protestants to Parliament. In affirming the obscenity of the pamphlets, Chief Justice Cockburn

This contribution is based upon earlier studies by the same authors. For documentation of the views expressed, the reader is referred to: Lockhart and McClure, *Literature, the Law of Obscenity, and the Constitution*, 38 Minn. L. Rev. 295 (1954); Lockhart and McClure, *Obscenity in the Courts*, 20 Law and Cont. Prob. 587 (1955); Lockhart and McClure, *Censorship of Obscenity: The Developing Constitutional Standards*, 45 Minn. L. Rev. 5 (1960); McClure, Book Review, 59 Col. L. Rev. 387 (1959). See also Paul and Schwartz, *Federal Censorship: Obscenity in the Mail*, especially pp. 191–204, 292–299 (1961).

framed a new legal test for obscenity—a test that was promptly adopted by courts in both England and the United States. The Lord Chief Justice, in the course of his opinion, remarked:

> I think the test of obscenity is this, whether the tendency of the matter charged as obscenity is to deprave and corrupt those whose minds are open to such immoral influences, and into whose hands a publication of this sort may fall.

He also spoke of depraving and debauching their minds and of corrupting their minds and morals. Although he did not explain what he meant by these words, he did express his conviction that the pamphlet in question 'would suggest to the minds of the young of either sex, or even to persons of more advanced years, thoughts of a most impure and libidinous character'. The suggestion of impure and libidinous thoughts, then, is the key to what depraves, debauches, and corrupts the minds and morals of the young and even the old, and so makes matter obscene.

As Chief Justice Cockburn's view of obscenity developed in the United States, impure and libidinous thoughts came to be regarded as so noxious, either of themselves or because of their supposed corrupting effect, that material could be condemned as obscene if any part might suggest such thoughts in the minds of the young and weak, regardless of the literary or other social values of the material viewed as a whole. And so the Hicklin case came to stand for the 'partly obscene' and 'most susceptible persons' tests for obscenity which at an early date became firmly imbedded in American law and were even inserted in the obscenity statutes of a number of states.

Slowly, however, opposition to these harsh tests for obscenity began to develop. In 1913 Judge Learned Hand spoke out against them although at the time they were so firmly established that he felt constrained to apply them in a criminal prosecution for the mailing of Daniel Carson Goodman's *Hagar Revelly*. After overruling a demurrer to the indictment, Judge Hand entered his now-famous protest against the Hicklin rule:

> . . . I hope it is not improper for me to say that the rule as laid down, however consonant it may be with mid-Victorian morals, does not seem to me to answer to the understanding and morality of the present time. . . . I question whether in the end men will regard that as obscene which is honestly relevant to the adequate expression of innocent ideas, and whether they will not believe that truth and beauty are too precious to society at large to be

mutilated in the interests of those most likely to pervert them to base uses. Indeed, it seems hardly likely that we are even today so lukewarm in our interest in letters or serious discussion as to be content to reduce our treatment of sex to the standard of a child's library in the supposed interest of a salacious few, or that shame will for long prevent us from adequate portrayal of some of the most serious and beautiful sides of human nature. . . .

Yet, if the time is not yet when men think innocent all that which is honestly germane to a pure subject, however little it may mince its words, still I scarcely think that they would forbid all which might corrupt the most corruptible, or that society is prepared to accept for its own limitations those which may perhaps be necessary to the weakest of its members. If there be no abstract definition, such as I have suggested, should not the word 'obscene' be allowed to indicate the present critical point in the compromise between candour and shame at which the community may have arrived here and now? . . . To put thought in leash to the average conscience of the time is perhaps tolerable, but to fetter it by the necessities of the lowest and least capable seems a fatal policy.

Yet, despite the persuasiveness of Judge Hand's vigorous criticism of the 'partly obscene' and 'most susceptible persons' tests for obscenity, it was not until the early 1930's that American courts generally began to reject them.

After a few preliminary skirmishes, the major attack on these two tests for obscenity came with the celebrated *Ulysses* case of 1933 and 1934, in which James Joyce's monumental work was cleared of an obscenity charge. In the United States District Court, Judge John M. Woolsey explicitly rejected the 'most susceptible persons' test for obscenity, saying that the book 'must be tested by the court's opinion as to its effect on a person with average sex instincts—what the French would call *l'homme moyen sensuel*—who plays, in this branch of legal enquiry, the same role of hypothetical reagent as does the "reasonable man" in the law of torts and "the learned in the art" on questions of invention in patent law.' He assumed that the book was to be judged as a whole, not by isolated passages ripped out of their context. In the Circuit Court of Appeals, Judge Augustus N. Hand explicitly rejected the 'partly obscene' test for obscenity, saying that 'the proper test of whether a given book is obscene is its dominant effect' and that the 'question in each case is whether a publication taken as a whole has a libidinous effect'. He assumed that the book was not to be judged by its effect upon unusually susceptible persons. But neither Judge Woolsey nor Judge Hand challenged the basic tenet of the Hicklin case that the stimulation of sexy thoughts is what makes material obscene. Indeed, both judges spoke of 'lustful thoughts' as if the stimulation of such thoughts were basic to an obscenity finding. Both judges also left some clues to the kinds of material that sufficiently promoted lustful thoughts to be classed obscene, for they both spoke of pornography, Judge Woolsey of 'dirt for dirt's sake', and Judge Hand of material that portrayed 'filth for its own sake'.

Although most American courts after *Ulysses* rejected the 'partly obscene' and 'most susceptible persons' tests for obscenity, there remained some parts of the country in which these tests were rigorously applied. Of these, Detroit, Michigan, was the most extreme. There, until 1957, more than a hundred books were censored simply because an assistant county prosecutor thought that he wouldn't want his very young daughter to read some passages the books contained. In 1957, however, the United States Supreme Court finally put an end to these two tests for obscenity: both, the Court declared, are unconstitutional.

The Court, however, did not invalidate all obscenity censorship. Nor did it question the 'libidinous thoughts' tenet of the Hicklin case. Instead, in the Roth–Alberts majority opinion, Mr Justice Brennan wrote that 'obscenity is not within the area of constitutionally protected speech or press' because it is 'utterly without redeeming social importance'. 'Obscene material,' he declared, 'is material which deals with sex in a manner appealing to prurient interest,' which he explained in a footnote was 'material having a tendency to excite lustful thoughts.' And a constitutionally satisfactory test for obscenity is the test adopted, he said, by American courts in relatively recent decisions: 'Whether to the average person, applying contemporary community standards, the dominant theme of the material taken as a whole appeals to prurient interest.'

This test for obscenity the Court borrowed from a tentative draft of the American Law Institute's *Model Penal Code*, but the Court and the Institute did not agree on its meaning. To the Institute, 'prurient interest' is a 'shameful or morbid interest in nudity, sex or excretion'; it is 'an exacerbated, morbid, or perverted interest growing out of the conflict between the universal sexual drive of the individual and equally universal social controls of sexual activity'. According to the Institute, material appeals to this interest when, of itself, it has 'the capacity to attract individuals eager for a forbidden look behind the curtain of privacy which our customs draw about sexual matters'. The Institute's primary purpose in adopting this test for obscenity was to prevent the exploitation of psychosexual tensions created by the conflict between the individual's normal sexual curiosity and drive, ana the powerful social and legal inhibitions that restrain overt sexual behaviour.

The Institute explicitly rejected the 'libidinous thoughts' tenet of the Hicklin case in both of the ways in which that tenet had been developed by American courts. To some American courts the tendency of material to stimulate sexy thoughts is enough to make the material obscene. To others, however, the stimulation of sexy thoughts alone is not enough; it is the tendency to deprave and corrupt by means of sexy thoughts that makes material obscene. And both of these tests for obscenity the Institute rejected. It rejected the first 'because it is unrealistically broad for a society that plainly tolerates a great deal of erotic interest in literature, advertising and art, and because regulation of thought or desire, unconnected with overt misbehaviour, raises the most acute constitutional as well as practical difficulties'. And it rejected the second because of the lack of evidence of any connection between obscenity and overt misbehaviour and 'the wide disparity of strongly held views as to what does tend to produce that result'. To the *Code*'s draftsmen 'it seemed obvious that enquiry as to the nature of the appeal of a book, *i.e.*, the kind of appetite to which the purveyor is pandering, is quite different from an enquiry as to the *effect* of a book upon the reader's thought, desire or action'.

But what seemed obvious to the draftsmen of the *Code* was not obvious to the Court. For after borrowing the phrase 'appeal to prurient interest' from the *Code*, the Court went on to say that 'material which deals with sex in a manner appealing to prurient interest' is 'material having a tendency to excite lustful thoughts', and that 'we perceive no significant difference between the meaning of obscenity developed in the case law and the definition of the A.L.I., Model Penal Code. . . .' So at this stage in the development of the American law of obscenity we are left with at least three disparate rationales for obscenity censorship based upon assumptions of social evils in: (1) stimulating sexy thoughts and desires regardless of their impact on overt behaviour; (2) overt sexual misbehaviour induced by the stimulation of sexy thoughts and desires; and (3) exploitation of psychosexual tensions by appealing to prurient interest.

But there are two more closely related rationales seldom spelled out by American courts but certainly of immense influence upon their decisions. These are derived from: (4) the community standard suggested by Judge Learned Hand in his early protest against the

Hicklin rule and (5) the pornography, dirt and filth mentioned by Judges Woolsey and Augustus N. Hand in the *Ulysses* case. And the current trend of American law seems to be in the direction of the last of these five rationale—pornography. For when we examine carefully what the United States Supreme Court has actually *done* and disregard what it has *said* about obscene material we find that the concept of pornography best explains the Court's actions.

In the term immediately following the Roth–Alberts cases the Court, in three *per curiam* decisions, unanimously reversed without opinion three United States Court of Appeals decisions that had upheld censorship of material found obscene by the trial courts. The Court did not send the cases back for new trial or reconsideration. Instead, it flatly reversed the judgments, citing the Roth case for authority, and thus put an end to the censorship then and there. The records in these cases, and the issues raised on appeal, make it reasonably clear that the only ground upon which the decisions could have been based was the Court's conclusion that the materials censored were not obscene. And these materials included the nudist magazines *Sunshine & Health* and *Sun*, a homosexual magazine entitled *One*, and the French motion picture *The Game of Love*. The nudist magazines contained numerous photographs plainly showing male and female genitalia and pubic areas; the homosexual magazine catered to the tastes and interests of homosexuals without living up to its declared purpose of dealing with homosexuality from a scientific, historical or critical point of view; and the motion picture depicted a series of illicit sexual relations between a young boy and an older woman and a girl of his own age.

Shortly after these *per curiam* decisions were handed down, three of the United States Supreme Court justices gave still another example of the kind of material that in their judgment cannot be classed obscene. In the Kingsley Pictures case of 1959 a majority of the Court reversed New York's censorship of the motion picture *Lady Chatterley's Lover* on the ground that New York could not censor films portraying acts of sexual immorality as 'desirable, acceptable, or proper patterns of behaviour'. But Justices Harlan, Frankfurter and Whittaker in a separate concurring opinion found that New York's censorship of the film was based upon 'actual scenes of a suggestive nature'. These included scenes showing the gamekeeper helping Lady Chatterley unbutton her blouse and unzip her dress, reaching under her dress to caress her buttocks and note that she had come to him wearing no undergarments, and lying in bed in a state of undress before and after the consummation of their love. Nevertheless, these justices concluded, the film is not and cannot be classed obscene.

But these applications of whatever may be the United States Supreme Court's concept of obscenity only tell us what in the Justices' opinion obscenity is not; they do not tell us what they think obscenity is. Thus far we can infer only that the Court's concept of obscenity is a very narrow one indeed, far narrower than most American courts have viewed obscenity in the past. For an indication of the positive concept of obscenity held by most members of the Court we have to return to the Roth–Alberts cases in which, we are convinced, the Court applied a concept of obscenity even though the obscenity of the materials disseminated by Roth and Alberts was not in issue.

The Roth and Alberts cases both reached the United States Supreme Court at a very high level of abstraction. The sole issue before the Court was whether the federal and California obscenity statutes, on their faces and in a vacuum, were constitutional. With the cases in this posture, the United States Solicitor General moved swiftly to bring them back to earth. He did so by arguing that the federal statute had to be held constitutional because it was necessary to prevent the country from being flooded with a mass of hard-core pornography, which, he said, constituted 90% of the material caught by the statute. The validity of the statute, he contended, had to be judged 'by this mass of "hard-core" pornography, which . . . is its main objective and its major catch'. He described hard-core pornography as erotic objects, photographs, books, and movies depicting men and women in 'every conceivable kind of normal and abnormal sexual relations' and 'excesses', and then pointed out that such material is produced solely for and solely produces erotic effect, that the only 'idea in hard-core pornography is that there is pleasure in sexual gratification, whatever the means', and that 'the social value of such notions is, of course, nil'. And to make sure that the Court really understood the nature of hard-core pornography, the Solicitor General sent to the Court a carton containing numerous samples and in an accompanying letter pointed out their 'extremely repulsive nature' and again reminded the Court that at least 90% of the convictions under the federal statute were for dealing in material of this kind.

In voting to sustain the constitutionality of the federal and California obscenity statutes, the Justices must have had material of this kind in mind, for hard-core pornography, particularly in pictorial form, is so blatantly shocking and revolting that it must have been impossible for them to put it out of mind. To give free circulation to such repulsive material in the name of constitutionally protected freedom of expression must to the Justices have seemed intolerable. Consequently, in this setting—none of which clearly appears in the opinions in the Roth–Alberts cases—the Court's rejection of obscenity as material 'utterly without redeeming social importance' takes on new and significant meaning. For it suggests that the Court's primary concept of obscenity is that of hard-core pornography, a concept that the New York Court of Appeals has since made explicit. Whether the United States Supreme Court will also limit obscenity statutes to hard-core pornography remains to be seen, but the enormous difficulty of drawing the line elsewhere makes that course of action highly probable. The United States Department of Justice must share this opinion, for it has recently abandoned its efforts to censor Henry Miller's *Tropic of Cancer*.

With this sketchy account of developments in the American law of obscenity in the background, we are perhaps ready to undertake a critical consideration of the various rationales that have been advanced for the censorship of obscenity. These rationales, we have seen, are five in number: (1) Sexy thoughts; (2) Overt sexual misbehaviour; (3) Exploitation of psychosexual tensions; (4) Community standards; and (5) Pornography.

Sexy thoughts. Following the Hicklin case most American courts seized upon Chief Justice Cockburn's reference to the suggestion of impure and libidinous thoughts as a basis for obscenity censorship. Many of them, however, overlooked a possible further step in his reasoning, for he spoke of the material's tendency to deprave, debauch and corrupt the minds and morals of its readers by means of suggested impure and libidinous thoughts, thus indicating a distinction between impure and libidinous thoughts and their depraving and corrupting consequences. In ignoring this further step in the Chief Justice's reasoning these American courts spoke as if material could be censored as obscene simply because it suggested sexy thoughts and without any explicit consideration of whether such thoughts would have a deleterious effect upon character or overt behaviour.

Despite their emphasis upon the stimulation of sexy thoughts as the basis for obscenity censorship, these courts never quite made clear exactly what kinds of thoughts and desires they wanted to protect persons from.

Employing a wide range of colourful terminology, they spoke of material that would allow, suggest, stir, arouse, implant, excite or incite impure, lecherous, libidinous, lustful, sensual, or sexual thoughts, desires and imaginations.

But what kinds of thoughts, desires, imaginations and impulses are impure, lecherous, libidinous, lustful, sensual or sexual? Do these words embrace thoughts of normal sexual intercourse? If so, within wedlock or only without? Or do they embrace only thoughts of sexual perversions?

Courts answered only the last of these questions clearly. They did so, not by an explicit consideration of the question, but by finding obscene many materials that dealt only with normal sexual relations and that could not possibly have suggested thoughts of sexual perversion. Only a few courts dealt with the second question; in cases involving the distribution of sex instruction and birth control books to a restricted audience of persons having a proper interest in the material, they found the books not obscene. Most courts, however, gave no hint that they had ever considered this basic question. To them, apparently, material that suggested sexual thoughts in any form could be found obscene.

There must, of course, be some causal relationship between the material and the sexy thought. But what degree of causal relationship is required? Is it enough that the material merely allows the thought to arise or suggests it? Or must the material stir, arouse, implant, excite or incite the prohibited thought?

Despite the obvious importance of these questions, most courts failed to recognise that there was any problem of causal relationship in obscenity cases. Only a very few discussed the problem. One court, holding that a sexual instruction pamphlet for adolescents was not obscene, remarked that the statute did not bar 'everything which *might* stimulate sex impulses' and that any 'incidental tendency to arouse sex impulses which such a pamphlet may perhaps have is apart from and subordinate to its main effect'. In a later case, the same court suggested that the degree of likelihood of sexual stimulation as well as the degree of intensity of the resulting sexual thought must outweigh the merits of the material. This court seems to have been primarily concerned with balancing the merits of the material against the likelihood and degree of its sexual stimulation and, in doing so, recognised that some sexual materials may be more stimulating than others. But even this court did not fully appreciate the complexity of the problem. Paul and Schwartz, summing up the results of some controlled studies of erotic responses to material, note that 'there is empirical evidence that the same erotic material may have a quite different effect on different persons and a quite different effect on any particular person, depending on where, when and how he is exposed to the material'.

Granting the fact that some kinds of material stimulate erotic responses in some persons in varying degrees depending on the nature of the material, the kinds of persons exposed to it, and the setting in which the exposure takes place, why should we censor such material solely because it stimulates sexy thoughts and desires?

Of the American courts that followed the sexy thoughts rationale for obscenity censorship, none ever explicitly answered this question. Instead, they tacitly assumed that sexy thoughts and desires were a sufficient evil in and of themselves to justify the censorship of material that stimulated such thoughts and desires. But where they acquired this notion is not at all clear. Perhaps it came from the religious principle that lustful thoughts are as sinful as lustful deeds. In any case, while it may be entirely appropriate for a church to discourage its adherents from material that turns the mind from spiritual to carnal thoughts, it would be wholly inappropriate for the government, under the American constitutional system, to impose a regime of censorship solely for the purpose of directing citizens' minds away from the physical interests of life towards more spiritual and worthy thoughts.

The stimulation of normal sexual thoughts and desires, moreover, is neither in itself immoral nor contrary to commonly accepted standards of behaviour. Sexual thoughts are perfectly natural; without them, men and women would be abnormal or subnormal. Indeed, the stimulation of such thoughts, even creating the desire for normal sexual intercourse, may sometimes be in the public interest. For example, Judge John M. Woolsey, in ruling that Dr Marie C. Stopes's *Married Love* was not obscene, remarked that the book had 'as its whole thesis the strengthening of the centripetal forces in marriage, and instead of being inhospitably received, it should, I think, be welcomed within our borders'.

Finally, the sexy thoughts rationale for obscenity censorship, rigorously followed, would destroy most erotically realistic literature. It certainly had that effect for a long time in the United States. In 1917 H. L. Mencken, then editor of the *American Mercury*, described the difficulties he faced as a practical editor:

. . . I find that the Comstocks, near and far, are oftener in my mind's eye than my actual patrons. The thing I always have to decide about a manuscript offered for publication, before ever I give any thought to its artistic merit and suitability, is the question whether its publication will be permitted —not even whether it is intrinsically good or evil, moral or immoral, but whether some roving Methodist preacher, self-commissioned to keep watch on letters, will read indecency into it. Not a week passes that I do not decline some sound and honest piece of work for no other reason. I have a long list of such things by American authors, well-devised, well-imagined, well-executed, respectable as human documents and works of art—but never to be printed in mine or any other American magazine. It includes four or five short stories of the very first rank, and the best one-act play yet done, to my knowledge, by an American. All of these pieces would go into type at once on the Continent; no sane man would think of objecting to them; they are no more obscene, to a normal adult, than his own bare legs. But they simply cannot be printed in the United States, with the law what it is and the courts what they are.

The sexy thoughts and desires rationale for obscenity censorship is, in our judgment, indefensible.

Overt sexual misbehaviour. After the Hicklin case not all American courts seized upon Chief Justice Cockburn's reference to the suggestion of impure and libidinous thoughts, finding in that reference the basis for obscenity censorship. Some of them noted the further step in his reasoning and ruled that material was obscene because it tended, by stimulating sexy thoughts, to deprave, debauch and corrupt the minds and morals of those exposed to the material. Although these words are not wholly free from ambiguity, they suggested something far more serious than the stimulation of a fleeting sexy thought or desire. For they indicated that material was obscene because of its deleterious effects upon character and overt sexual behaviour.

If there were any dependable way to ascertain the probable effects of sexual material upon the character and overt sexual behaviour of persons exposed to the material, most of the difficulties of obscenity censorship would be solved. Measuring the probable resultant behaviour against current community standards in sexual matters would provide a rational and defensible criterion for obscenity censorship. Despite the great importance of freedom of expression, there could be little doubt of the constitutional validity of censoring material that demonstrably is likely to induce persons exposed to the material to engage in overt sexual misbehaviour. But no method has yet been devised to forecast the probable effect of sexual materials upon overt sexual behaviour; for psychiatrists, psychologists and other social scientists have so far failed to provide us with any reliable basis for determining what causal relationship, if any, exists between exposure to sexual material and overt sexual misbehaviour. Paul and Schwartz sum up the psychiatric comment on the issue, as follows:

> ... The psychiatric sources do seem to teach that one effect of reading or viewing erotic or shocking material may be the stimulation of fantasies—fantasies which are, at least in part, the product of unconscious, perhaps repressed, sexual or aggressive urges. The feelings thus evoked obviously may have more impact on the behaviour of a sexually 'maladjusted' adult or juvenile—the individual who already has difficulty in handling sexual or aggressive impulses. Some psychiatric authorities seem to believe that the fantasies and feelings evoked by exposure to erotic stimuli will often trigger a release of the maladjusted person's suppressed feelings; the release may simply take the form of a sort of psychic masturbation or perhaps, also, physical masturbation and nothing more; indeed, some authorities have even asserted that this kind of 'release' is beneficial for persons with strong, suppressed impulses because the experience operates as a 'safety valve' for 'deviates' or 'potential offenders'. But other authorities seem to believe that the fantasies and ensuing stimulation may, in some cases, produce aggressive conduct; thus the experience of exposure to 'obscene' stimuli is asserted by some to be a factor causing harmful misbehaviour *among already maladjusted persons*; but precisely how this stimulation works, and the extent to which obscenity, apart from the many other influences and stimuli, can trigger harmful external conduct, seem most unclear. Indeed, there is apparently some question whether, if 'obscenity' were unavailable, a less erotic stimulus would not be used to achieve the same effect. A few authorities seem to suggest that materials depicting extreme violence and sadism may suggest—teach, in an intellectual sense—ideas and methods for misconduct to deviate persons; and, in this sense, it has also been asserted that obscenity is a 'cause' of dangerous behaviour. Again, of course, the thesis, even if true, is limited to the impact of some forms of obscenity on a small class of readers who are admittedly already prone to misconduct. Whether obscene writings and pictorial matter can be singled out as *sine qua non* scapegoat remains controversial. None of the psychiatric assertions is based on statistical evidence; all are simply clinical judgments.

Surely, the current state of the social sciences is such that empirical studies of the relationship between erotic material and overt sexual behaviour can be made. Certainly, the need is there. But the practical difficulties of designing and conducting such studies are enormous, and it may be a long time before we have any reliable evidence. Meanwhile the overt sexual misbehaviour rationale for obscenity censorship seems too slender a reed to lean upon.

Exploitation of psychosexual tensions. In drafting its *Model Penal Code* the American Law Institute rejected the 'sexy thoughts' and 'overt sexual misbehaviour' rationales for obscenity censorship; both were found wanting. In their place, the Institute set up a new rationale: the exploitation of psychosexual tensions by appeals to prurient interest. To this end, it drafted a new definition of obscenity: 'A thing is obscene if, considered as a whole, its predominant appeal is to prurient interest, i.e., a shameful or morbid interest in nudity, sex or excretion, and if it goes substantially beyond customary limits of candour in description or representation of such matters.' And it went on to say that the material must be judged by its impact upon ordinary adults unless aimed at an audience of children or other specially susceptible persons.

But this new rationale for obscenity censorship is not without its own difficulties, similar in many respects to the difficulties that led the Institute to reject the 'sexy thought' and 'overt sexual misbehaviour' rationales for obscenity censorship.

The first of these difficulties seems to stem from a problem of communication. We have already seen that the United States Supreme Court could see no material difference between the Institute's and the 'sexy thoughts' rationales for obscenity censorship. Nor can we say precisely how the two rationales differ, for many ordinary adults manifest considerable curiosity about sexual material that may stimulate sexy thoughts and some interest in taking an occasional 'forbidden look behind the curtain of privacy which our customs draw about sexual matters'. Of perhaps greater significance, however, is the fact that, trying as hard as we are able, we cannot clearly envisage the kinds of sexual material the Institute's rationale and definition of obscenity would censor. Would they catch nudist magazines? Girlie magazines? If so, how extreme would they have to be? Would they catch such books as Henry Miller's *Tropic of Cancer?* In short, what inroads would the Institute's rationale make into the publication and dissemination of erotically realistic literature that had literary value, great or small? Perhaps the draftsmen of the *Model Penal Code* could furnish answers to these questions, but we cannot. And we do not see how courts would be able to do so, either.

C

Apart from the problem of communication, the Institute's rationale raises some fundamental questions. Why should the exploitation of psychosexual tensions be prevented? Is their exploitation a sufficiently serious social evil to justify invoking the power of the state to censor obscenity as defined in the *Code*? Does all of the material embraced by the *Code's* definition of obscenity actually exploit psychosexual tensions? What effect does the tension or anxiety have upon the personality or overt behaviour of persons exposed to such material? To these fundamental questions we have no answers. And until social scientists address themselves to these questions and come up with some reliable answers, it seems clear that the Institute's rationale for obscenity censorship seems to be almost as slender a reed to lean upon as the 'overt sexual misbehaviour' rationale.

Community standards. The community standards rationale for obscenity censorship has been appearing with increasing frequency in the American judicial opinions and legal literature dealing with the law of obscenity. We have already noted the reference to community standards in the American Law Institute's *Model Penal Code* and in Mr Justice Brennan's majority opinion in the Roth–Alberts cases. But in referring to community standards, courts and commentators have not always had the same concept in mind, a diversity probably due to the inherent ambiguity of the concept.

What 'community' may be used as the touchstone for obscenity? Is it a community bounded by geographical limits or a community formed along social or cultural lines? If a geographical community, is it a local community, and, if local, how local—a particular state, urban or rural area? Or is it the national community or even the larger international community commonly called the western world?

What 'standards' of the community may be applied? Are they the standards of any particular social or cultural subcommunity within a given geographical community? Are they the particular moral standards held or at least voiced by most members of the community? Or are they, like the taboos of primitive societies, the community's culturally established outer limits of tolerance?

At the present stage in the development of the American law of obscenity, only a few of these questions can be answered with assurance. Since the Kingsley Pictures case, in which the United States Supreme Court ruled that New York could not constitutionally censor motion pictures simply because they portrayed acts of sexual immorality as 'desirable, acceptable or proper patterns of behaviour,' we know that what has been called 'ideological obscenity'—material that is critical of currently held or voiced moral standards—may no longer be censored as obscene for that reason alone. This, we take it, precludes the community's particular moral standards as a criterion of obscenity; it also suggests that the community's 'standards' are its culturally established outer limits of tolerance for sexual expression. The constitutionality of the 'most susceptible persons' test for obscenity, which Mr Justice Frankfurter once likened to burning the house to roast the pig, leads us to the further conclusion that the standards of a particular social or cultural subcommunity may not be employed to censor material for other groups within a larger geographical community; it also suggests that the 'community' whose standards may be applied as a criterion of obscenity is a geographical one rather than a community formed along social or cultural lines. And we are convinced, for reasons too lengthly to set out in this essay, that the geographical community is a national one rather than particular state or local communities.

If the 'community' is a national community and its 'standards' are its culturally established outer limits of tolerance for sexual expression, it seems clear that under the 'community standards' rationale the only material beyond the pale is hard-core pornography, for this is the only class of material that contemporary American society as a whole utterly rejects and simply will not tolerate. There appears to be no national consensus upon sexual material that falls short of that line. Which leads us, of course, to a consideration of the 'pornography' rationale for obscenity censorship.

Pornography. We have noted that the United States Supreme Court's primary concept of obscenity is probably one of hard-core pornography and that the New York Court of Appeals has recently and explicitly adopted hard-core pornography as the sole test for obscenity censorship in that state. But what is 'hard-core pornography' and why do we want to censor it?

Dr Margaret Mead, the noted anthropologist, gives us one of the best explanations of pornography available. She says that pornography is material 'calculated to stimulate sex feelings independent of the presence of another loved and chosen human being', that its 'essential element' is 'the daydream as distinct from reality'. According to Dr Mead:

... (T)he material of true pornography is compounded of daydreams themselves, composed without regard for any given reader or looker, to stimulate and titillate. It bears the signature of nonparticipation—of the dreaming adolescent, the frightened, the impotent, the bored and sated, the senile, desperately concentrating on unusualness, on drawing that which is not usually drawn, writing words on a plaster wall, shifting scenes and actors about, to evoke and feed an impulse that has no object: no object either because the adolescent is not yet old enough to seek sexual partners or because the recipient of pornography has lost the precious power of spontaneous sexual feeling.

Margaret Mead's conception of pornography as daydream material calculated to feed the auto-erotic desires of the immature, the perverted and the senile is supported by the Kronhausens's detailed analysis of pornographic books in *Pornography and the Law*. For they found in pornographic books the same sexual fantasy that Dr Mead emphasised. Pornographic books, they observe, are always made up of a succession of increasingly erotic scenes without distracting non-erotic passages; their sole purpose is to stimulate erotic response, never to describe or deal with the basic realities of life.

Many psychiatrists have also noted in pornography its essential daydream quality, designed to feed the erotic fantasies of the sexually immature. D. W. Abse says that pornography 'simply encourages people to luxuriate in morbid, regressive, sexual-sadistic phantasy'. W. G. Eliasberg speaks of pornography's appeal to 'immature sexuality', which he describes as a 'non-genital, not individualised, not-loving, amorphous interest in sex'. London and Caprio note that those who collect pornography 'have a libido that is fixated at the paraphiliac level', a level of 'psychic auto-eroticism'. And Benjamin Karpman calls indulgence in pornography a form of psychic masturbation.

So analysed, pornography as a concept assumes manageable form. It is daydream material, divorced from reality, whose sole purpose is to nourish the erotic fantasies of the sexually immature or, as the psychiatrists say, psychic auto-eroticism. It provides a reasonably satisfactory tool for distinguishing most pornographic material from the non-pornographic. As applied to some kinds of material, however, it is not likely to be as successful, for much widely distributed and accepted material—such as the 'pin-up girl'—is designed to serve much the same function, yet is seldom attacked as obscene. If materials of this kind are to be excluded, the qualification 'hard-core' needs to be appended to 'pornography' to indicate that the material must not only have as its sole purpose the nourishment of the erotic fantasies of sexually immature persons but must be grossly shocking as well.

But why should we censor pornography, hard-core or otherwise? What significant social evil are we trying to guard against? What is so terribly wrong about erotic fantasy and the dissemination of material—even shocking material—that feeds the sexually immature person's craving for such fantasy? After all, people in the western world have been dreaming for hundreds of years about a mythical land of Cockagne which W. H. Auden describes as the land 'Where whiskey-rivers run / And every gorgeous number may / Be laid by anyone'. Yet Margaret Mead takes a very grave view of the problem saying:

> Pornography does not lead to laughter; it leads to deadly serious pursuit of sexual satisfaction divorced from personality and from every other meaning. . . . The difference between the music hall in which a feeble carrot waves above a bowl of cauliflower while roars of laughter shake the audience of husband(s) and wives on their weekly outing, and the strip tease, where lonely men, driven and haunted, go alone, is the difference between the paths to heaven and hell, a difference which any society obscures to its peril.

Some psychiatrists have argued that for some adolescents, at least, pornography is harmful. Exposed to pornography, particularly of the hard-core sado-masochistic type, they may be led to become sexual perverts or deviates and even to engage in acts of criminal violence. Others have said that indulgence in pornography arrests sexual development, suggesting that exposure to pornography may permanently stunt or retard the growth of some persons into sexually mature human beings. Still others have noted that, for some maladjusted persons, indulgence in pornography serves as a release for tensions that otherwise might produce more serious consequences. But these observations are, at best, clinical judgments and informed guesses, and we find ourselves once again with too little reliable information to support a rationale for obscenity censorship. As before, though the need for reliable knowledge is great, social scientists have not as yet sufficiently addressed themselves to the problem to give the information we need to form a rational basis for obscenity censorship.

Until that far-off day when the social sciences have been able to furnish enough reliable knowledge to form a rational basis for obscenity censorship, perhaps the best we can do is to do what we might have to do anyway—to admit that in our way we are as bound by our culture as the members of primitive societies are in their way, that in our culture there are outer limits of tolerance for sexual expression, and that a combination of the 'community standard' and 'pornography' rationales for obscenity censorship serves our immediate needs about as well as any. Limiting the material that may be censored as obscene to hard-core pornography—material whose sole purpose is to nourish the sexually immature person's craving for erotic fantasy and in addition is so grossly shocking as to exceed the community's outer limits of tolerance—would restrict the dissemination of materials of the kind social scientists are most likely to find have harmful social effects and at the same time free art and literature from the fetters of an irrational and unduly restrictive obscenity censorship. This may come to no more than saying, as Zecharia Chafee once noted, '"We will permit what we will permit," which is going around in a circle,' but for the time being it is the best we can do.

LORD BIRKETT

The Changing Law

THE words which are used as the title of this book—To Deprave And Corrupt—are taken from the celebrated judgment of Chief Justice Cockburn in the case of Reg. *v.* Hicklin in 1868. That judgment laid down the test of obscenity in English law, as it continued to be the test until it was amended by the Obscene Publications Act of 1959. In Hicklin's case the words are:

> The test of obscenity is whether the tendency of the matter charged as obscenity is to deprave and corrupt those whose minds are open to such immoral influences and into whose hands such a publication might fall.

In Clause I (I) of the Obscene Publications Act 1959 the words are:

> For the purposes of this Act an article shall be deemed to be obscene if its effect or (where the article comprises two or more distinct items) the effect of any one of its items is, if taken as a whole, such as to tend to deprave and corrupt persons who are likely, having regard to all relevant circumstances, to read, see or hear the matter contained or embodied in it.

While the definition in the Act is more liberal and reasonable, it still contains the words 'tend to deprave and corrupt' which have been and are likely to be the cause of much trouble in interpretation when particular cases come before the courts. The words have recently been the subject of discussion in the House of Lords in the case of Shaw *v.* Director of Public Prosecutions (1961 Weekly Law Reports, p. 897) and to that case I shall return at a later stage. One of the purposes of this book is to discuss the law relating to obscene or pornographic publications and matters connected therewith; but it is quite impossible to consider the law of obscenity without raising the much larger question of the law's connection with literature, and the written word in general; and with the powers of control which, for good or ill, the law has exercised in days past and which it still exercises today. The law of England at all times has been very closely concerned with the rights of the individual, and with the liberty of the individual in particular. But the freedom of thought and expression enjoyed today has been won at great cost and is only to be preserved by continued vigilance. Both statute law, and what may be called judge-made law, have been equally concerned with the spoken and the written word. From 1538 to 1695, for example, a series of decrees and statutes imposed a system of licensing upon the printing and publishing of books, pamphlets and the like; and the judges were responsible for the creation of a new law in 1727 whereby it became an offence at common law to publish what was called an obscene libel. That common law misdemeanour remained a very active part of English law until it was repealed by the Act of 1959 to which I have already referred.

It is now universally agreed that any kind of control or censorship on the publication of the written or the spoken word, however imposed, is a restriction on the liberty of the individual; but it is also recognised that some control is necessary in any civilised community. But such control can only be justified if its purpose is to prevent harm or injury either to the individual, the general public, or to the good order of the community. If it is imposed under colour of these things when no such conditions exist, or if it is maintained when any such necessity has vanished, it is an evil thing and ought to be abolished.

I do not speak of totalitarian countries where governments repress all freedom of expression for their own purposes and without that regard for the individual which has been characteristic of English life for many centuries; but it is not possible to be complacent in England about the need to preserve true liberty in the matter of the spoken and written word as the criminal prosecutions that were brought in 1954 against publishers of the highest standing very markedly emphasised, though to speak truly there is in 1961 an enlightened and educated public opinion fully aware of the need for vigilance. Some famous words used by Erskine in the eighteenth century when defending the publisher Stockdale who was charged with uttering a libel on the House of Commons at the instance of Charles James Fox might well be remembered at all times:

> From minds thus subdued by the terrors of punishment, there could issue no works of genius to expand the empire of human reason, nor any masterly compositions on the general nature of government by the help of which the great commonwealths of mankind have founded their establishments. Under such terrors all the great lights of science and civilisation must be extinguished; for men cannot communicate their free thought to one another with a lash held over their heads.

It was the recognition of the immense power contained in the written word that caused governments to impose the restrictions of which

Erskine spoke and which today causes the dictators and tyrants to continue to do so. It was the fear of the written word which impelled governments in the eighteenth century to resort to prosecutions based on the law of 'constructive treason' in order to defeat the public demand for parliamentary reform, and the acquittals of Hardy, Horne-Tooke and Thelwall on such charges marked a notable stage in the fight for liberty of expression.

There is one further observation I would wish to make at this stage about the English law and freedom of expression. Generally speaking, the law is expected to be in accordance with the ideas and beliefs of the age in which it is operative. Sometimes it lags behind and sometimes it races ahead, but if the law is radically out of touch with prevailing ideas it will not win willing obedience to its decrees. When the penalty for stealing in a shop to the value of five shillings was death without benefit of clergy, as it was in the year 1700, judges, juries and counsel all conspired together to defeat what was felt to be a monstrous barbarity, and the most valuable goods were valued by juries at four shillings and elevenpence, and judges quashed indictments for the mere mis-spelling of a name. This factor of the beliefs and ideas of the age must never be lost sight of when reviewing the history of English law. That great American judge—Benjamin Cardozo—said in his famous book on *The Nature of the Judicial Process*:

> My duty as a judge may be to objectify in law not my own aspirations, convictions and philosophies, but the aspirations, convictions and philosophies of men and women of my time

and further—

> . . . Logic and history and custom and utility and the accepted standards of right conduct are the forces which singly or in combination shape the progress of the law. Which of these forces shall dominate in any case, must depend largely upon the comparative importance or value of the social interests that will thereby be promoted or impaired . . . and if you ask how is he to know when one interest outweighs another, I can only answer that he must get his knowledge just as the legislator does, from experience and study and reflection; in brief, from life itself. Here indeed is the point of contact between the legislator's work and his.

It is still a very surprising thing to reflect, for example, that there was a time in England when it was laid down as law by a court of quite exceptional knowledge and ability that a property owner was not obliged to perform a contract to let a set of rooms after he had discovered the rooms were to be used for a Rationalist lecture under the auspices of the Liverpool Secular Society. Yet in 1867 three learned Barons of the Exchequer held that the purpose of the letting was unlawful because the denial of the truths of Christianity was a violation of law for Christianity was part and parcel of the law of England.[1] There was also a time in England when an agreement between a husband and wife to live apart would not be an enforceable agreement, because the minds of men and judges were governed by considerations which have long lost all validity. It is wise therefore to look upon past ages with some sense of toleration, and to examine closely the reasons which influenced governments to make their statutes, and judges to make their decisions in this highly controversial field of the Spoken and the Written word.

The control which is imposed to prevent injury to the public or to the state is usually political or moral censorship of one kind or another. So far as the written word is concerned no form of control had very much importance until the invention of printing in Europe in the fifteenth century. That tremendous happening which changed the course of history brought with it immense problems, some of which were quickly seen, and some which only developed in the course of time. Some of those problems still persist. The invention of printing was first hailed by the government as a thing to be encouraged in every possible way.

But by the sixteenth century, and after some notable books had been printed by Caxton at Westminster, restriction of various kinds and systems of censorship had already become firmly established. In 1553, the Statute of Henry VIII was the forerunner of the later legislation which imposed the system of licensing which was to endure until the closing years of the seventeenth century. The Statute was designed ostensibly to protect the printers who it was said were highly-skilled craftsmen and capable of producing all the printed matter the country required without any importations from the continent of Europe. But five years later the Star Chamber issued the first Licensing Decree, and thenceforward the power to grant licences to print any book or pamphlet became part of the Royal Prerogative, that is to say, it became one of those rights which the King alone enjoyed as distinct from all his subjects, and the common law had long declared that this was the essential feature of the Prerogative. It was now obvi-

---

[1] Cowan v. Milbourn. 1867 Law Reports 2 Exchequer. p. 230.

ous, of course, that this great new invention of printing could be made
a source of great profit for the Crown, and at the same time the power
to control the printing of books and pamphlets and the like enabled
the government to exercise the greatest influence over the expression
of public opinion by stifling all opposition to any government
proposal. This control was exercised through the Court of Star
Chamber, that Court which existed from 1487 to 1641 sat in a
room at the Palace of Westminster and on the ceiling of that
room stars were painted from which the name of the Star Chamber is
derived.

The name has many evil associations and the good which the Court
undoubtedly did in those lawless and unsettled times is apt to be overlooked. Its origin is interesting. From very early times, when the law
was very far from being settled, some decisions were made by the
King himself sitting with his Privy Council to advise him. In course
of time the King ceased to attend himself and the task of judgment
was then exercised by the Privy Councillors themselves. Quite soon
another important change took place. The Privy Council divided into
two parts, one part being concerned with matters affecting the government of the country as a whole, and the other part dealing with purely
legal questions, and usually the most difficult and complicated legal
questions. It was this legal part of the Privy Council, which always
contained some judges, that became the Court of Star Chamber by
virtue of the Statute of 1487 and exercised what were called the King's
power of reserve judgments. The Court had many demerits—the use
of torture, the denial of the most elementary justice to individuals
accused before it, the complete subservience to the King and the like—
but its action in exercising the King's prerogative in the matter of
printing and publishing effectively controlled the free expression of
opinion. Although its first Decree in 1538 appears not to have been
enforced, it yet set the pattern for future decrees and for the Statutes
that followed. The important thing was that nobody in England could
print any book or pamphlet unless the Privy Council had first examined it and given its approval to the printing. The incorporation of
the Stationers' Company was a tremendously important event and a
most ingenious one so far as the control of printing was concerned.
From very early times there had been in existence *The Craft of Writers
of the Text Letter*, and as early as 1403 they had applied successfully to
the Court of Aldermen for authority to elect Wardens and make rules
for their own government. They had their stalls or stations round

about St Paul's and, because of this, when the Company was incorporated in 1556 it took the title of the Stationers' Company. The purpose of the Crown was twofold. It was primarily to prevent the publication of seditious books in opposition to the government, and heretical books in opposition to the Church. The new Stationers' Company was given the monopoly of printing (save in a few special cases) and in return the Company undertook to search for and then to suppress illegal books of the kind mentioned. The Wardens were given immense powers. They could destroy the books and sentence all offenders to imprisonment. In addition they could and did impose heavy fines and shared the proceeds with the Crown. The Charter was confirmed by Elizabeth I and the rigid censorship by means of licensing was sternly enforced. The first Act of Parliament, as distinct from a Decree, was the Act of 1633 and its purpose was to prevent the printing of those writings the authorities regarded as seditious or heretical. The Act was renewed from time to time, but in 1695 the House of Commons refused to renew it, and the system of licensing came to an end and has never been revived. Milton's *Areopagitica*, the famous plea for the liberty of unlicensed printing, apparently went quite unheeded, for the refusal of the House of Commons to renew the Act was not made until twenty-one years after Milton's death and fifty-one years after the publication of *Areopagitica*. The main reason why the Act was not renewed had nothing to do with the freedom of the press although of course it had that effect. The House of Commons refused to renew the Act partly because the monopoly of the foreign book trade in the Port of London was felt to be unfair, and partly because the strict observance of the Act was becoming very difficult to enforce. But it seems to be the view of the historians that during this long period of Licensing the interests of literature had not greatly suffered. It was during this period that Francis Bacon published the *Advancement of Learning* with the matchless praise of books:

> But the images of men's wits and knowledges remain in books, exempted from the wrong of time, and capable of perpetual renovation. Neither are they to be fitly called images, because they generate still, and cast their seeds in the minds of others, provoking and causing infinite actions and opinions in succeeding ages. . . .

Men of letters and men of science had used the printing press to publish many works of lasting value. Newton's *Principia* was published in 1686–87 and bore the imprimatur of Samuel Pepys as President of the

Royal Society. During this period, too, Milton published *Paradise Lost* and Bunyan published *The Pilgrim's Progress*.

It is interesting to note that under the Act of 1663 political works were licensed by the Secretary of State, law books by the Lord Chancellor, books on Heraldry by the Earl Marshal, and all other publications by the Archbishop of Canterbury and the Bishop of London. After 1696 of course a man might print and publish anything he chose subject to the ordinary laws of the land, which, at that time, included very severe laws relating to Sedition and Blasphemy. Down to the year 1854 all questions of fact in the common law courts were decided by juries, but in libel the judges had always taken the view that the question of whether words constituted a libel was a question of law for the judge, and the jury were only concerned with publication. Lord Mansfield had taken this view as early as 1770 in certain cases arising out of the printing of the famous letters of Junius, but in 1792 Fox's Libel Act became law and after that date, libel or no libel was a question for the jury. It will have been observed that obscenity and pornography have little place in the law until the eighteenth century. Down to the year 1727 obscenity was punished, if at all, by the ecclesiastical courts, and those punishments were excommunication and the like. The abolition of licensing seems to have given a fillip to pornographic writing and it did not take long for protests to be made about it. In the case of Bowman *v.* Secular Society Ltd. in 1917 Lord Sumner said:

> The time of Charles II was one of notorious laxity both in faith and morals, and for a time it seemed as if the old safeguards were in abeyance or had been swept away. Immorality and irreligion were cognisable in the Ecclesiastical courts, but spiritual censures had lost their sting and those civil courts were extinct which had specially dealt with such matters viewed as offences against civil order. The Court of King's Bench stepped in to fill the gap.

In 1663 Sir Charles Sedley had exposed himself on a balcony in Covent Garden and had actually made water on the people below and had thrown bottles down on to the crowds that gathered. There appears to have been much doubt whether his conduct, other than the bottle-throwing, was such that the King's Bench could deal with it though it was submitted that 'this court is *custos morum* of all the King's subjects and it is high time to punish such profane conduct'. But in 1708 in the case of Reg. *v.* Read, where the defendant had published a pornographic book and indeed made a trade of so doing, Mr Justice Powell dismissed the case saying there was no law to punish it. In 1727, however, where a man named Curle had published a pornographic book, the Attorney-General of the day submitted that the publication was an offence at common law because 'it tends to corrupt the morals of the King's subjects and is thus against the peace of the King'. This submission was accepted with some hesitation because there was no open breach of the peace as in Sedley's case, and the new offence, the common law misdemeanour of publishing an obscene libel, became part of the law of England and remained so until the passing of the Obscene Publications Act 1959 when the law was re-cast.

In giving judgment in Curle's case Lord Raymond, C.J., said:

> If it reflects on religion, virtue or morality, if it tends to disturb the civil order of society I think it is a temporal offence.

Throughout the eighteenth century pornographic publications increased and public opinion was growing in strength that they should be suppressed or controlled. Midway through the nineteenth century a very important statute was passed called the *Obscene Publications Act 1857* sometimes known as Lord Campbell's Act. It provided a summary procedure (which has been much strengthened in the Act of 1959) whereby obscene publications might be searched for by the police and brought before justices who had power to order the destruction of offending publications if the case was properly made out. When the Bill was discussed in the House of Lords both Lord Brougham and Lord Lyndhurst criticised it on the ground that it would be injurious to literature, to which Lord Campbell replied that it was not within his most distant contemplation that works of literature should be affected at all. The Bill was aimed exclusively at those who have the single purpose of corrupting the morals of youth or of shocking the conscience of reasonably minded people.

And in 1868 the case of Reg. *v.* Hicklin was heard, first before the justices, then on appeal to Quarter Sessions, and finally to the Queen's Bench Division of the High Court. It was in that court that the test of obscenity was laid down which was quoted at the beginning of this chapter. There the words 'to deprave and corrupt' occur and for nearly a hundred years they have been used as though their meaning was quite clear, whereas their true interpretation is still a matter of acute difficulty as evidenced by the recent discussion in the House of Lords in Shaw's case. In 1949 the *Sunday Times* called public attention to a

book and urged its immediate withdrawal on the ground of its extreme obscenity. After much public discussion the Attorney-General of
the day said in answer to questions in the House of Commons that
'there are two public interests to which I must have regard. It is important that no publisher should be permitted to deprave or corrupt
public morals, to exalt vice, or to encourage its commission. It is also
important that there should be the least possible interference with the
freedom of publication and that the Attorney-General should not seek
to make the criminal law a vehicle for imposing a censorship on the
frank discussion or portrayal of sordid and unedifying aspects of life
simply on the grounds of offence against taste or manners.' That
reasonable statement met with wide approval, for it said in effect, 'Let
pornography perish but let literature have the necessary freedom.' In
the year 1954 there were a series of prosecutions against highly reputable publishers some of which resulted in convictions, some in disagreement of the jury and some in acquittals. Much depended on the
way the judge left the case to the jury. In the case where the publishers
were Messrs Secker and Warburg, who had published a book called *The
Philanderer*, the judge was Mr Justice Stable. After having directed the
jury to read the book 'as a whole' he summed-up the case to them with
great liberality of mind. He was careful to say that the test of obscenity
was the test laid down in Hicklin's case and then examined the words
'to deprave and corrupt' in relation to the conditions of the present
day and made the clearest distinction between obscenity and pornography. The summing-up is well known and two short quotations will
indicate the enlightened view of the judge. He said:

> Your verdict will have a great bearing upon where the line is drawn
> between liberty and that freedom to read and think as the spirit moves us,
> on the one hand, and on the other, a licence that is an affront to the society of
> which each of us is a member.

On the important words 'to deprave and corrupt' the judge said:

> Remember the charge is a charge that the tendency of the book is to
> corrupt and deprave. The charge is not that the tendency of the book is
> either to shock or disgust. That is not a criminal offence. Then you say:
> 'Well, corrupt or deprave whom?' and again the test; those whose minds are
> open to such immoral influences and into whose hands a publication of this
> kind may fall. What exactly does that mean? Are we to take our literary
> standards as being the level of something that is suitable for a fourteen-year
> old schoolgirl? Or do we go even further back than that, and are we to be

reduced to the sort of books one reads as a child in the nursery? The answer is of course not. A mass of literature, great literature, from many angles is wholly unsuitable for reading by the adolescent but that does not mean that the publisher is guilty of a criminal offence for making those works available to the general public.

The jury acquitted the defendant and a pretty strong blow had been struck for freedom of expression. It must be emphasised that Mr Justice Stable accepted the Hicklin test as law, but had interpreted the Statute in the light of contemporary thought. But he did not alter the law, and judges were not compelled to follow his liberal example. In the September following this notable summing-up, the then Recorder of London summed-up to a jury at the Old Bailey in a very different fashion although the judgment of Mr Justice Stable was quoted to him at some length. But public opinion in the literary world had been greatly stirred, and as a result the Obscene Publications Act 1959 came into being, which declares that on a charge of publishing an obscene article no man shall be convicted if it is shown that the publication in question is justified as being for the public good, on the ground that it is in the interests of science, literature, art or learning, or of other objects of general concern.

The concern of the government with religion and morals has always been deep and is still so at the present day. At common law it is still an indictable misdemeanour to speak or otherwise publish any matter blaspheming God, e.g., by denying His existence or providence or contumeliously reproaching Jesus Christ or vilifying or bringing into disbelief or contempt or ridicule Christianity in general or any doctrine of the Christian religion or the Bible or the Book of Common Prayer. For at least two hundred and fifty years the law of England as propounded by the judges was that the doctrines of Christianity were part of the common law of England. To assert the contrary was to assail the very foundations of ordered society. In 1797 when the publisher of Tom Paine's *The Age of Reason* was prosecuted and convicted of publishing a blasphemous libel because the book alleged that the Old Testament had served to brutalise and corrupt mankind by its accounts of savage conduct and the like, Mr Justice Ashurst in sentencing the publisher said: 'All offences of this kind are not only offences to God but crimes against the law of the land . . . inasmuch as they tend to destroy those obligations whereby civil society is bound together; and it is upon this point that the Christian religion constitutes part of the law of England.' But forty-five years later the law had undergone a great change as public opinion had altered, and in 1842 Mr Justice Coleridge could say, 'There is nothing at common law that is unlawful in reverently doubting or denying doctrines parcel of Christianity, however fundamental' and after another forty years Chief Justice Coleridge could say—'I now lay it down as law that if the decencies of controversy are observed, even the fundamentals of religion may be attacked without the writer being guilty of blasphemy.' But it was not until 1917 in the case of Bowman *v.* Secular Society Ltd that the House of Lords laid down the law finally and authoritatively and illustrated once more the need for the law to be in accordance with the ideas of the age. Lord Sumner said in that case:

> The words, as well as the acts, which tend to endanger society differ from time to time in proportion as society is stable or insecure in fact, or is believed by its reasonable members to be open to assault. . . . In the present day reasonable men do not apprehend the dissolution or downfall of society because religion is publicly assailed by methods not scandalous. . . . After all the question whether a given opinion is a danger to society is a question of the times and a question of fact . . . experience having proved dangers once thought real to be now negligible, and dangers once very possibly imminent to have now passed away, there is nothing in the general rules as to blasphemy and irreligion, as known to the law, which prevents us from varying their application to the particular circumstances of our time in accordance with that experience.

Sometimes the change in the law is made by statute as in The Children an¹ Young Persons (Harmful Publications) Act 1955 which was aimed at the alarming increase of what were called 'Horror Comics' and in the Obscene Publications Act 1959 to which I have referred. But the power exercised by the judges to bring the law into conformity with the ideas and feelings of the age is still exercised and is still exceedingly important. It must always be kept in mind that much of the English law is still the common law where it has not been superseded by statute. For example, at common law, all open lewdness, grossly scandalous, and whatever openly outrages decency or is offensive and disgusting, or is injurious to public morals by tending to corrupt the mind and destroy the love of decency, morality and good order is a misdemeanour indictable at common law. Which leads me to the latest case concerning these matters, the case of Shaw *v.* Director of Public Prosecutions.

That case shows a remarkable cleavage of opinion and the dissenting opinion of Lord Reid may yet be ranked with the dissenting judgment of Lord Atkin in Liversidge *v.* Anderson in 1942 on the construction of the words in Regulation 18B of the war-time Defence Regulations. The case of Shaw is a lengthy one and ought to be read in full because it illustrates and illuminates many things and most particularly the difficulty of deciding what the words 'to deprave and corrupt' are expected to mean when circumstances may differ so widely, and when evidence of depravity and corruption following on the reading of any publication is naturally difficult if not impossible to obtain. What is regarded as offensive or degrading or obscene differs greatly in different ages and in different grades of society.

What then is the proper direction for a judge to give to a jury in cases where obscenity is charged? When criminal cases are tried by juries, their decisions are much affected by the guidance given to them by the judge. How widely and how quickly the ideas of one age may differ from another can be seen in a case such as the prosecution of Charles Bradlaugh and Mrs Annie Besant. They were charged with publishing obscene matter in 1877 when all that they had done was to publish an exceedingly well-written pamphlet advocating birth control. The Solicitor General of the day, afterwards the Lord Chancellor, described the publication as filth, yet for many years now such literature is paid for and published by local authorities and is regarded by them as essential and beneficial knowledge, although some people still describe such matter as pornographic.

Shaw's case was an ordinary criminal case tried before a judge and jury at the Old Bailey in September 1960. The indictment contained three counts, the first being a charge of conspiracy to corrupt public morals, the second being a charge of living on the earnings of prostitution, and the third of publishing an obscene article, to wit, a publication called *The Ladies' Directory*. This Directory contained the names and addresses of women who were prostitutes together with a number of photographs of nude female figures. In his book, *Obscenity and the Law*, to which I am deeply indebted, as are all writers on this present theme, Mr St John-Stevas records that a similar publication entitled *List of Covent Garden Ladies* was published in 1780 and circulated freely without any action being taken by the authorities.

In Shaw's case the defendant admitted through his counsel at the Old Bailey that he published the Directory in order to assist prostitutes to ply their trade, when as a result of the Street Offences Act 1959 they could no longer solicit in the streets. Evidence was given before the jury by several prostitutes about how much they paid for the advertisements, about certain sexual perversions referred to in some of the advertisements and similar matters. No evidence was called by the Defence but certain submissions in law were made to the judge. It was submitted that there was no such offence in English law as a conspiracy to corrupt public morals, and that there was no evidence to support the charge made in the second count. The judge ruled against all the submissions and in summing-up to the jury he used these words:

> The test, therefore, that you have got to apply is laid down by the Act of Parliament—is the effect of this publication, taken as a whole, such as to tend to deprave and corrupt persons who are likely to read it. . . . If the effect of this document is thought by you to encourage or induce readers of it to resort to prostitutes for fornication and/or for the other deviations we have heard about, and if that is a thing which corrupts and depraves such people, and if you think they are then acting in a depraved and corrupt way, then in my view the effect of this article would be to tend to deprave and corrupt and it would be obscene within the definition of this Act. Whether to induce or encourage a person likely to read this article to resort to prostitutes for this purpose, does, in fact, tend to deprave and corrupt is of course a matter for you in the light of my previous observations to you on this subject.

Shaw was convicted on all three counts and sentenced to nine months imprisonment.

Shaw appealed to the Court of Criminal Appeal and the appeal was dismissed, but leave was given to go to the House of Lords on counts 1 and 2. The Court of Criminal appeal held that the offence of conspiring to corrupt public morals was a misdemeanour at common law and reviewed all cases from 1663 onwards. In the House of Lords Lord Simonds said.:

> I am concerned only to assert . . . that such an offence (conspiracy to corrupt public morals) is known to the common law and that it was open to the jury to find on the facts of this case that the appellant was guilty of such an offence. . . . We are perhaps more accustomed to hear this matter discussed upon the question whether such and such a transaction is contrary to public policy. . . . In the sphere of criminal law I entertain no doubt that there remains in the court a residual power to enforce the supreme and fundamental purpose of the law, to conserve not only the safety and order, but also the moral welfare of the State.

This view of Lord Simonds was supported by Lord Tucker, Lord Morris of Borth-y-Gest and Lord Hodson. Lord Hodson said:

> The judicial precedents which have been cited show conclusively to my mind that the courts have never abandoned their function as *custodes morum* by surrendering to the legislature the right and duty to apply established principles to new combinations of circumstances. . . . Even if Christianity is not part of the law of England yet the common law has its roots in Christianity and has always regarded the institution of marriage as worthy to be supported as an essential part of the structure of society to which we belong. I do not see any reason why a conspiracy to encourage fornication and adultery should be regarded as outside the ambit of a conspiracy to corrupt public morals.

Lord Morris said:

> There are certain manifestations of conduct which are an affront to and an attack upon recognised public standards of morals and decency, and which all well-disposed persons would stigmatise and condemn as deserving of punishment. The cases afford examples of the conduct of individuals which has been punished because it outraged public decency or because its tendency was to corrupt the public morals.

The dissenting speech of Lord Reid deserves to be read in full. It occupies several pages of the Law Reports and covers all the points raised in the case in the three courts before which the case came. But on the first count in the indictment he was of opinion that there is no such general offence known to the law as conspiracy to corrupt public morals. He was further of opinion that if a new offence was to be created it must be done by Parliament and not by the judges. On the meaning of the words 'to deprave and corrupt' Lord Reid said:

> I cannot find any intention to widen the old law of obscene libel or to make it possible for a prosecutor to charge as obscene libel publication in wholly inoffensive terms of any matter which tends to raise lustful desires in the mind of a reader whether that matter be allusion to or commendation of fornication or merely the name and address of a prostitute.

Lord Reid was of opinion that it is an indictable offence to say or do anything in public which outrages public decency whether or not it also tends to corrupt and deprave those who see and hear it. In Lord Reid's view it is open to a jury to hold that a public invitation to indulge in sexual perversion does so outrage public decency as to be a punishable offence; and a jury properly directed might have found Shaw guilty on this ground. Lord Reid concluded with these words:

> It has always been thought to be of primary importance that our law, and particularly our criminal law, should be certain: that a man should be able to know what conduct is and what is not criminal. . . . Some suggestion was made that it does not matter that this offence is very wide: no one would ever prosecute and if they did no jury would ever convict if the breach was venial. Indeed the suggestion went further: that the meaning and application of the words 'deprave' and 'corrupt' (the traditional words in obscene libel now enacted in the 1959 Act) or the words 'debauch' and 'corrupt' in this indictment ought to be entirely for the jury, so that any conduct of this kind is criminal if in the end a jury think it so. In other words you cannot tell what is criminal except by guessing what view a jury will take, and juries' views may vary and may change with the passing of time. . . . If the trial judge's charge in the present case was right, if a jury is entitled to water down the strong words 'deprave', 'corrupt', or 'debauch' so as merely to mean 'lead astray morally' then it seems to me that the court has transferred to the jury the whole of its functions as *censor morum* and the law will be whatever any jury may happen to think it ought to be. . . .

When I moved the Second Reading of the Obscene Publications Act 1959 in the House of Lords I said that I doubted whether any quite satisfactory act would ever get to the Statute Book dealing with obscenity and its various problems. Shaw's case, with the differences of view expressed, lends some support for that statement. But it must be remembered that in Shaw's case eight judges were of one view against one on the other side. The majority thought that the act of Shaw was to conspire with others to corrupt public morals, and that was an offence the law recognises and in proper cases punishes. It was not a decision in which the doctrine of 'public policy' was invoked. That doctrine has nothing to do with governments or government policy, but has been and still is invoked when judges feel it to be necessary, and in the past all decisions into which 'public policy' has entered have been for the most part decisions concerned with making all law harmonise with the moral law. Shaw's case was one where existing law was applied, and it must therefore be the law of England that the offence of conspiring to corrupt public morals exists, and that such an offence was committed in the circumstances of Shaw's case. The Law Lords in Shaw's case were concerned for the moral welfare of the state. Lord Radcliffe in his lectures to the Northwestern University at Illinois concluded his second lecture entitled *Riding an Unruly Horse*, a phrase used by an English judge in 1824 dealing with doctrines of 'public policy', with these words:

> It is a fine phrase 'the liberty of the law', if we only set ourselves to give it meaning. It was used long ago by Sheppard in his *Touchstone*; if a condition, he says, 'tends to provoke or further the doing of some unlawful act, or to restrain or forbid a man from the doing of his duty, the condition for the most part is void . . . hence also it is that such conditions as are against the liberty of law, as that a man shall not marry or the like, are void. And hence also such as are against the public good.

The public good demands that men should have freedom of expression, but it must be freedom governed by the law of the land.

NORMAN ST JOHN-STEVAS

The Church and Censorship

THE Christian Church has always paid books a high compliment by taking them seriously. Unfortunately this concern for literature has not always been regulated by counsels of prudence. The early Christians were deeply distrustful of the pagan world and this distrust led to edicts banning the reading of pagan works and often to the destruction of precious manuscripts. For such an attitude there were certainly precedents in antiquity. In China for example, Tsin Chi Hwangti, who built the great wall (214 to 204 BC), and was one of the country's greatest monarchs, conducted a crusade against books. We are told by Edmund Gosse that in 213 BC he 'attempted the extinction of all literature, root and branch, with the exception of those books dealing specifically with medicine, agriculture and science. Not only were the books burned, but five hundred of the *literati* who had offended him most were executed and banished.' There is nothing to parallel this in Christian history. Nevertheless books fared badly in early Christian hands. We read in the Acts of the Apostles that the Ephesians burnt their bad books at the instigation of St Paul, and this tradition was maintained by the early Christian Fathers. 'To read books subversive of religion', said St Isidore, 'is to offer incense to the devil.' St Augustine was equally uncompromising: 'By means of immoral matter nice language is not acquired but by means of nice language immorality is learned. I do not accuse the language but the intoxicating wine of error that we drink in from it.' At the beginning of the fourth century the Council of Carthage decreed that Christians were no longer to possess or distribute the writings of the old pagan authors. In 389 came the destruction of the Serapeum under an edict of the emperor Theodosius, carried out by the Christian bishop Theophilus. By a strange historical irony it was the Renaissance Popes who, centuries later, were to search out and cherish pagan manuscripts, but then they were not especially religious men.

The Church at times concerned itself with obscenity in literature, but the early Churchmen were much more worried about heresy and subversive philosophies. In 325 the Council of Nicea condemned the errors of Arius and proscribed his writings. The works of another heretic, Nestorius, were condemned at the Council of Ephesus in 431. In 496 Pope Gelasius issued a list of sixty books which were not to be read. Then the dark ages supervened and reading was reduced to such a minimum level that it no longer presented any kind of threat. In the Middle Ages there was no organised system of Papal censorship although books of individuals were from time to time condemned. For example in 1121 the works of Abelard were condemned, and in 1418 at the Council of Constance, those of Wyclif and Huss. But in an age when books were only to be found in manuscript form and read only by the learned, the Church was not especially alarmed about their effect even when they were opposed to her teaching.

The Church in Anglo-Saxon times and the Middle Ages was certainly not worried about obscenity, and writers were free to be as ribald as they pleased. In English literature obscenity makes an early appearance. The Exeter Book, the manuscript of which with that of Beowulf, the Vercelli Book and the Junian manuscript, form the earliest sources of Anglo-Saxon literature, contains a fine collection of obscene riddles.[1] These incredibly gross riddles were in fact lovingly collected by a monk and included in a work intended to be a work of piety. For the most part the Exeter Book is made up of devotional, penitential and didactic works. Mediaeval literature was as robust and uninhibited. Even those writers who had an explicitly didactic purpose did not hesitate to describe the vices they were denouncing in vigorous and vivid language. Ballads, the most popular form of literature, were frank, as were the lyrics of the thirteenth and fourteenth centuries. Chaucer, court poet though he was, was not an inhibited writer, as a reading of *The Miller's Tale* will remind, but contemporaries were not shocked. The pilgrims were not scandalised by the revelations of the Wife of Bath, and bawdiness was not considered incompatible with religious devotion. This broadmindedness was not confined to England: the fourteenth century, after all, was the century of the subsequently much-banned Boccaccio, who anticipated his critics in the Epilogue to his tales. 'Most noble damsels', he wrote, 'corrupt mind did never yet understand any word in a wholesome sense ... everything is in itself good for somewhat and being put to

---

[1] Anglo-Saxon Riddle No. 44.

'A strange thing hangs by a man's thigh under its master's clothes. It is pierced in front, is stiff and hard, has a good fixed place. When the man lifts his own garment up above the knee, he wishes to visit with the head of this hanging instrument the familiar hole which it, when of equal length, has often filled before.'

The answer to the riddle is of course 'key'.

a bad purpose may work manifold mischief. And so I say it is with my stories. If any man shall be minded to draw from them matters of evil tendency or consequence they will not gainsay him.' It is true that Savanarola threw *The Decameron* into his Florence bonfire in 1497, but he was a fanatic, untypical of his age. When *The Decameron* did finally come under the Papal ban in 1559 this was not because of the peccadillo of its obscenity but for the much graver offence of its satirising of the clergy. The Church authorised an expurgated edition, but the references expunged were those relating to the saints and the clergy; the obscenities remained. Accordingly monks became magicians, nuns were turned into noblewomen and the Archangel Gabriel transformed into the king of the fairies.

The Church in the later Middle Ages may have been easy-going about obscenity, but as her control over the minds of citizens began to be challenged so her reactions to heresy became more sharp. The problem of controlling heretical books in England arose during the fifteenth century in connection with John Wyclif. Wyclif was born in 1320 and died at Lutterworth in 1384. Two years earlier his views had been condemned at the Synod of Oxford (1382). On 10th March 1400 a statute was passed in order to suppress the Wyclifite heresy. The statute is of interest because of its reference to heretical books whose owners were required to deliver them up to the authorities. At the Oxford Synod of 1407, Archbishop Arundel drew up a series of provincial constitutions to control heretical books. The major of these constitutions were later embodied in an Act of Parliament, but two minor provisions not so favoured are worth noting. Constitution VI provided for a censorship of all books read at universities and in the schools. Constitution VII forbade any translation of the scriptures and also the reading of any such 'book, libel or treatise set forth in the time of John Wyclif or since, or hereafter to be set out'. In 1410 a statute was passed punishing those who wrote books against the Catholic faith.

The Lollard threat passed but was replaced by the greater menace of Lutheran books. On 17th July 1520 Leo X issued a Bull ordering the seeking out and burning of Lutheran books. In England, Cardinal Wolsey applied the Papal decree with zeal and in March 1521 the Pope wrote personally to thank him for his efforts. On 12th May 1521 Luther was formally declared a heretic from St Paul's Cross and his books were ordered to be burnt. Despite this, Lutheran books continued to circulate and sporadic attempts were made to suppress them. It should be remembered that heresy at this time was considered as much an offence against the state as against the Church, and the state was as anxious as the Church to suppress heretical books. Indeed the state often took the initiative. In 1538 Henry VIII introduced a royal licensing system. No English books were to be printed without a licence from the Privy Council. In particular no English translation of the Scriptures was to be printed unless licensed either by the King, the Privy Council or a bishop. Similar restrictions were placed on the importing of books. This decree marks the beginning of the Tudor Censorship, but it does not seem to have been strictly enforced. Throughout Henry's reign decrees were issued against heretical books. The breach with Rome made no difference as Henry was anxious to establish his orthodoxy and would brook no dissent. A new peril was added to the lives of printers by the Act of Six Articles which upheld the doctrines of transubstantiation and auricular confession among others, and anyone who attacked them by writing or printing was to forfeit his goods and the profits of his land for life, as well as being imprisoned at pleasure for the first offence. For the second, he was to be guilty of felony without benefit of clergy, which meant execution.

With the accession of Edward VI in 1547 this anti-Protestant policy was rescinded, but there was no freedom of printing conferred. The government's efforts were simply directed against Catholic instead of against Protestant books. Proclamations were issued against 'papisti-call' books, a new prayer book introduced, and orders for the destruction of the old service books sent out. All printing in English was to be licensed by one of three secretaries. The only difference made by the fall of Somerset was a proclamation which transferred the licensing to the Privy Council. Mary's accession in 1553 meant yet another reversal of policy, but the royal determination to control printing was unchanged. One of the first acts of her reign (18th August 1553) was to issue a proclamation forbidding any printing without a licence. This proclamation does not seem to have been especially effective, and another followed in 1555 condemning heretical works and giving royal officials powers of search and seizure. The service books of Edward VI were expressly banned. Despite these measures Protestant books continued to be printed and circulated. They bore fictitious imprints and although most were printed abroad, some were printed in England and some even in Ireland.

The Tudor system of censorship was religious and political, and the two cannot be separated. To hold a religion different from the sovereign was to be inclined towards sedition. *Cuius regio eius religio*, was an effective doctrine of politics. Yet despite this joining of the powerful forces of Church and state it was until 1556 remarkably ineffective. This was because of the lack of an effective instrument to enforce the royal wishes. The licensing system was unenforceable because the Tudors lacked a civil service and the officials of Star Chamber lacked the necessary knowledge of the printing trade to track down illegal printing and presses. In any case they were already overburdened with other tasks. It was Mary who in 1556 found the right instrument for enforcing the government will. She incorporated the Stationers' Company, the contemporary trade union of the printing trade, and gave it a monopoly of printing and a number of other privileges. In return for the charter, the members undertook to search out and suppress all undesirable and illegal books. This was a royal master stroke, and for the first time the system of licensing books made some approach to being effective. In 1559 the charter was confirmed by Queen Elizabeth after which she introduced, by decree, a system of licensing books, which was to last until 1695.

This system of licensing was used in defence of the established Church and the established government, and the Church was by this time of course the Church of England. But the Catholic Church had also devised a means of defending her doctrines, and although this had no effect in England it had a wide influence in many countries on the Continent. It is convenient at this point to turn away from the English scene and examine it. In the first part of the sixteenth century a number of countries had drawn up lists of heretical books which were to be banned. Charles V had composed such a list in Belgium in 1524. Venice produced a list in 1543 and the University of Paris in 1544. These were provincial and isolated efforts and it was not until Paul IV issued a list of books to the Inquisition in 1559 that any action was taken by the central spiritual authority. This led to the matter being brought before the Council of Trent which in 1564 issued the first comprehensive list of banned books which was afterwards to be known as the Index. The Index was to be a powerful weapon by which the Church both tried to hold the ground she was left with in Europe and to recover some of the territory she had lost. Given the traumatic shock that the Church had suffered at the Reformation and the paramount need to defend herself against disintegration the Index at the time was not an unreasonable institution. Whether it serves any useful purpose today is another matter.

Apart from issuing a list of heretical works the Council laid down ten rules to govern printing, publishing and reading of books. No book was to be published without the permission of the local bishop and the rules provided that all books treating 'ex professo' of obscene subjects should be banned. These rules lasted two hundred years until the pontificate of Benedict XIV. The Congregation of the Index, a group of cardinals and priests who were to supervise the application of the rules and to revise the list of banned books, was set up by Pius V and put on a permanent basis by the Bull *Sollicita ac Provida* (1753). Pius IX mitigated the rules in 1848 and a general reform was agreed upon. This resulted in the promulgation of new rules in 1897 and 1900 saw the issue of a new Index. The rules were further altered in the new code of canon law prepared by Pius X and issued by his successor Benedict XV in 1917. This is the system that is at any rate nominally in force in the Roman Catholic world today. It will be discussed later in this essay. At this point one must return to Elizabethan England.

The essence of the Elizabethan system was the co-operation between the Crown, the Church and the Stationers' Company. No book was to be printed unless first licensed by 'her maiestie by expresse wordes in writynge, or by vi of her priuy council or be perused and licensed by the archbysshops of Cantobury and Yorke, the bishop of London, the chauncelours of both unyuersities, the bishop beying ordinary, and the Archdeacon also of the place where any suche shal be printed, or by two of them, whereof the ordinary of the place to be alwaies one.' The decrees provided for the punishment of offenders and were addressed to the Company, which, as under Mary, acted on behalf of the Crown. Licensing fees were paid to the Company and every book printed was entered in the Company's Register. At the end of Queen Elizabeth's decree came an interesting provision: 'Prouyded that these orders do not extend to anye prophane [i.e. classical] aucthours and workes in any language that hath been heretfore commonly receyued or allowed in any the unyuersities or Scoles: But the same may be prynted and used as by good order they are accustomed.' *The Decameron* had been granted a reprieve.

The injunctions were as far as possible enforced and imprints such as 'seen and allowed' and 'set forth and allowed', according to the order in the Queen Majesty's injunctions, became common form. But even with the help of the Stationers' Company it was not easy to secure universal obedience to the decrees, and their constant re-issue by Star Chamber shows that they were avoided, and much secret printing and smuggling of books went on. The Papists and later the Puritans were the quarries of the government. Fr Persons set up a printing press on his arrival in England in June 1580, his printer being Brinkley who was seized with the press in 1581. Robert Southwell, the Jesuit poet probably had his own private press, and James Duckett was a well-known printer executed for printing Catholic books.

Later the government turned against the Puritans. Whitgift had become Archbishop of Canterbury in 1583 and although staunchly anti-Roman he was also a militant anti-Puritan. In 1586 he secured an extension of the censorship powers from the Star Chamber. No printing was to take place except at London and at Oxford and Cambridge, and no new printing presses were to be set up without the permission of the Archbishop of Canterbury and the Bishop of London. In October 1588 came the first of the Marprelate tracts attacking the bishops with a broad scurrility. 'Printed oversea, in Europe', proclaimed the tract, 'within two furlongs of a Bounsing Priest, at the cost and charge of M. Marprelate, gentleman.' Seven tracts were issued before the government finally put an end to them.

The Tudor ecclesiastical licensing system was political and theological, not moral, and hence the licensers did not on the whole interfere with literature, nor save in extreme cases did they withhold licences because books were obscene. In the records of the Stationers' Company there are only a few isolated references to the censoring of books for obscenity. Yet popular literature was certainly registered. The following is a typical entry: 'Recevyd of William Coplande for his lycense for printinge of a ballett intituled "the lamentation of an olde man for maryinge of a yonge mayde etc."' Stubbes thought the licensers were lax and complained of the delay in licensing serious works while other books 'full of all filthiness, scurrility, baudy, dissoluteness . . . are either quickly licensed or at least easily tolerate'. Elizabethan Puritans disapproved of bawdy books, but their efforts were concentrated against the stage, and the Marprelate controversies absorbed much of their energies. In 1580 W. Lambard published a corrected draft of 'An Act of Parliament for the Establishment of the Governors of the English Print'. These 'governors' were to be eight members of the Inns of Court and no printing was to take place without their licence. The 'Act' remained a dead letter and was never presented to Parliament. The ecclesiastical courts were no more zealous than the prerogative courts in punishing cases of obscenity. There are very few reported cases of punishment for obscenity and in those there

D

is nearly always an element of defamation which until the sixteenth century fell within the ecclesiastical jurisdiction.

Under James I and Charles I the ecclesiastical censorship grew more severe but the Stuarts, like the Tudors, left literature free. The zeal with which the decrees were enforced varied with the personality of the reigning Archbishop of Canterbury. Archbishop Bancroft succeeded to the see in 1604, and until 1610 pursued a policy of suppression. His successor George Abbot held more moderate views and the decrees were not so rigorously enforced. In 1627, after the accession of Charles I, he was deprived of his office because of his moderation. After Abbot had been sequestered, Charles appointed a commission of four bishops and Bishop Laud, then Bishop of Bath and Wells, to exercise the archiepiscopal jurisdiction. From that time onwards Laud's influence steadily increased. In 1629 he became Bishop of London, and four years later Archbishop of Canterbury, the result being an ecclesiastical censorship of a strictness hitherto unknown in England. The royal and ecclesiastical will was enforced through the prerogative courts. Before the dissolution of Charles I's third parliament and the beginning of period of personal rule, the sentences of those found guilty of printing offences had been mild; after the dissolution they became more severe. In 1630, for example, Alexander Leighton was summoned before the Star Chamber for his book *Sion's Plea Against Prelacy*. In it he denounced Buckingham as Goliath, the Queen as Jezebel, and the bishops as 'wrens and magpies' and 'knobs and wens of bunchy popish flesh'. He was degraded from his office, sentenced to life imprisonment in the Fleet, ordered to be pilloried and whipped, his ears to be cut off, his nose split, and his cheeks branded. He escaped from custody after sentence but was recaptured and the orders of the court carried out. In 1641 he was awarded compensation for his sufferings by the House of Commons.

Another victim was Richard Blagrave who was arrested for stocking forbidden books. The records of the Court of High Commission record that on 19th April 1632, 'Richard Blagrave being imprisoned for having taken into his house many new Bibles of the Geneva print with the notes, and among divers other bookes these two libells come over from Amsterdam, and he was accused to be one that had a stocke going in the trade. He was brought to the Court and petitioned shewing that those bookes were all leaft at his house by one John Evans, a Factor, and sould him for an old debt, and he denyeth that he hath any stocke going in the trade, or that he sent for these bookes over, and prayeth to be released. He is committed till he bring forth Evans.'

A comic interlude was provided by the arraignment of Barker and Lucas, the King's printers, for their errors in printing the 'wicked' bible. On 8th May 1632 the High Commission rolls record: 'Mr Barker, the printer. There is a cause begunne against him for false printeing of the Bible in divers places of it, in the edition of 1631, vizt. in the 20 of Exo(dus) "Thou shalt commit adultery"; and the fifte of Deut(eronomy), "The Lord hath shewed us his glory, and his great asse"; and for divers other faults; and that they had printed it in very bad paper. And the BISHOP OF LONDON shewed that this would undoe the trade and was a most dishonourable thing: that they of the Church of Rome are soe carefull, that not a word or a letter is to be found amisse in their Ladie's Psalter and other superstitious bookes: and that we should not be soe carefull in printinge the sacred Scriptures: and that they in Holland at Amsterdam, had gott up an English presse and had printed the Bible in better paper, and with a better letter, and can undersell us 18d in a bible. Mr Barker and his partners endeavoured in partt to excuse themselves, and had advocates to speak for them, and were willing to submitt, and promised to amend their faults; but the Court would not remitt their offence, but the cause was ordered to goe on.' On 18th February 1633 Barker was fined £200 and Lucas £100 for their negligence. Other fines recorded on that day were £3000 to be paid by Lady Eleanor Davis, the mad sister of the notorious Lord Castlehaven, for publishing fanatical pamphlets: 100 marks to be paid by William Pamplin for dispersing Popish books: and £30 and £23 to be paid respectively by William Brooks and Blomfield for a similar offence.

On 7th February 1633/4 William Prynn was brought before the Star Chamber to answer for his book *Histrio-mastix*. Since 1627 Prynn had been prominent for his attacks on Arminianism and although the government had tried to arrest the circulation of his books its efforts had not met with great success. In *Histrio-mastix*, however, he had gone too far, and it was alleged that he had attacked the Queen. Prynn was sentenced to imprisonment for life, fined £5000, expelled from Lincoln's Inn and disbarred, sentenced to the pillory and ordered to lose his ears. The sentence was not fully carried out, but the book itself was vigorously tracked down. The limitations of government control were shown by the fact that Prynn continued to issue pamphlets despite his confinement in the Tower. More and more antigovernment and anti-Church tracts came from the presses and in a vain attempt to establish control the Star Chamber resorted to even more savage penalties. In 1637 Prynn was sentenced to be branded with the letters S.L. (seditious libeller), to stand in the pillory and to lose his ears. This time the sentence was carried out and the executioner cut off Prynn's ears very close to the head. He became a popular martyr. Despite his and other arrests, Puritan books continued to circulate in London and elsewhere, the domestic sources being supplemented by imported books from Holland. In a final effort to establish an effective censorship a new decree regulating printing was issued by the Star Chamber on 11th July 1637. The partnership between the government and the Stationers' Company was maintained, but the licensing provisions were made more detailed than in the Elizabethan decree. Importing of seditious or heretical books was already forbidden, but the decree laid down a new regulation. Before any of the books were offered for sale or circulated the importer was to present 'a true catalogue in writing of all and euery such booke and bookes vnto the Lord Arch-Bishop of CANTERBURY, or Lord Bishop of LONDON for the time being vpon paine to haue and suffer such punishment for offending herein, as by this Court, or by the said High Commission Court respectiuely, as the seueral causes shall require'. The number of printers was also restricted by the decree.

The projected system of censorship was certainly worthy of the exponents of the policy of 'Thorough'. Every loophole in previous decrees had been closed, and had it been possible to enforce the new provisions, an effective censorship would have been established. This, however, was what the government could not do. Apart from the intrinsic difficulty of the task they had set themselves, Charles, Laud and Strafford were entangled in pressing problems of both domestic and foreign policy. The personal rule was about to break down and in 1639 Charles became involved in war with Scotland over the new prayer book of 1637. In 1640 in order to obtain funds for the war Charles was obliged to recall Parliament. The 'Short Parliament' was soon dissolved, but on 3rd November 1640 'The Long Parliament' met in London. An immediate attack was launched on the royal prerogative, the King's ministers and the instruments of his government. The Star Chamber was abolished in 1641 and with it fell the whole royal system of licensing of books, for it had been built up on the prerogative, not by statute. At the same time, High Commission and the ecclesiastical courts were done away with. Printing thus enjoyed a brief period of complete freedom. It was not to last for long.

Parliament authorised sporadic prosecutions of seditious printers, but the flood of books and pamphlets was so great that in March and June 1643 general ordinances were issued which regulated the book trade and re-introduced full scale censorship. The second decree moved Milton to write his *Areopagitica* in which he conceded that certain books should be proscribed, but condemned a general censorship. But Parliament was set on a general censorship and turned again to the Stationers' Company to help it enforce its will. Licensing was required as under the Stuarts and special licensers were appointed by Parliament. The law was now used in the Puritan interest, but owing to the unsettled state of the country and the outbreak of civil war—Charles had raised his standard at Nottingham in 1642—the censorship was much less effective than in former times. The position was further complicated by divisions within the Puritan ranks such as the split between the Presbyterians and the Independents in 1644 which led to an increase in secret printing. John Lilburne and Richard Overton made full use of secret presses to attack the Presbyterian divines. Richard Overton continued to operate his press until 31st July 1646 when he was arrested and the press seized. After the end of the civil war royalist publications continued to be published and Parliament published further ordinances to control printing and this was followed by an Act of Parliament in 1649. The Council made strenuous efforts to enforce the Act, but unlicensed printing continued. A new Act was passed in 1653 and for a time rigorously enforced. Within two months, eighteen printers had been committed either to Newgate or the Gatehouse for printing pamphlets attacking Cromwell. On 13th January 1654 a general search warrant was issued to the Sergeant-at-Arms and as a result of his activities London was strewn with broken printing presses. Despite these and other efforts unlicensed printing continued as before. In April 1660 Prynn, whose position had moderated, was chosen by the Commons to draw up an Act to deal with the control of the printing trade, but before he could report the King had returned.

Charles II had no more intention than Cromwell of allowing freedom of printing, and at once set about devising means to control it. The task was more difficult than ever owing to the growth of the press since 1641. The phenomenal increase in newsbooks, newsletters and pamphlets had made the problem of controlling publication more urgent and at the same time had made it more complicated. Star

Chamber and High Commission had gone which made the Crown's task more difficult. However, in 1662 a new Licensing Act was passed by Parliament. All printing without a licence was forbidden: power was given to search premises and to seize any unlicensed books that might be found there: the number of master printers was limited to twenty. The religious and political purpose of the Act can be seen from the text of its first section: 'No person shall presume to print etc. any heretical, seditious, schismatical or offensive books or pamphlets wherein any doctrine or opinion shall be asserted or maintained which is contrary to the Christian faith, or the doctrine and discipline of the Church of England, or which shall or may tend or be to the scandal of religion or the Church, or the government or governors of the Church, State or Commonwealth, or of any corporation or particular person or persons whatsoever.' Different officials were designated as licensers for different subjects. Books of divinity, philosophy or medicine were to be licensed by the Archbishop of Canterbury, the Bishop of London, or the Chancellor or Vice-Chancellor of one of the universities. Every book was to carry the licence in front of the text. A copy was to be retained in the licenser's hands so that any subsequent changes in the book could be detected. 'Upon the said Copy licensed to be imprinted he or they who shall so license the same shall testifie under his or their hand or hands that there is not anything in the same contained that is contrary to Christian Faith or the Doctrine or Discipline of the Church of England or against the State or Government of this Realme or contrary to good life or good manners or otherwise as the nature and subject the Worke shall require, which License or Approbation shall be printed in the beginning of the same Booke with the Name or Names of him or them that shall authorise or license the same for a Testimony of the allowance thereof.' In addition every copy was to bear the name of its printer. Further clauses regulated the importing of books. Merchants were to import books into London only; to present a catalogue to the Archbishop; and not to open packages unless a duly appointed person was present, together with a member of the Stationers' Company. Extensive powers of search were conferred on royal officials. 'Provided alwaies that no search shall be att any time made in the House or Houses of any of the Peers of this Realm or of any other person or persons not being free of or using any of the Trades in this Act before mentioned, but by special Warrant from the Kings Majestie under the Sign Manual or under the Hand of one or both of His Majesties principal Secretaries of State, or for any other

Books then such as are in printing or shall be printed after the Tenth of June one thousand six hundred and sixty two, anything in this Act to the contrary thereof in any wise notwithstanding.' A year after the passing of the Act the Secretaries created the office of Surveyorship of the Press, whose occupant was to be charged with the control of the Press under their general direction. On 15th August 1633, Roger L'Estrange was appointed to the office.

L'Estrange found as much difficulty in enforcing the licensing provisions as his predecessors. He fought with the Stationers' Company and succeeded in getting their rules reformed in 1678. These regulations, if enforced, might well have proved an effective check on illegal printing, but before they could be made effective England became engulfed in the Popish Plot. The consequent wave of illegal printing was too strong for the Company to turn back, and the government was left to cope with it as best it could. The regulations marked the end of the Company as an independent force, and since it was unable to give the government effective aid, it has no further importance in the history of censorship. In May 1679 the Licensing Act expired and was not renewed. Theoretically the press had become free, but with the Crown already engaged in its struggle with Shaftesbury and the Exclusion Bill controversy still having to be fought out, the government was in no mind to allow its opponents unrestricted liberty of expression. To achieve its end the Crown turned to the common law judges who supplied the necessary support. This was of short-lived duration and led to the impeachment of the Chief Justice.

Charles II died in 1685 and was succeeded by his brother James, whose first Parliament revived the Licensing Act. Under William and Mary the Licensing Act remained in force at first. It should have expired in 1692/3, but a new statute extended it for a further two years. In 1695 a committee of the House of Commons recommended that the Licensing Act should be continued, but when the motion was put to the House it was defeated. Parliament then allowed the Licensing Act to lapse. In doing this the Commons was not striking a blow for the liberty of the press but expressing its conviction that the Act had failed to achieve its purpose. On 3rd May 1695, the Licensing Act finally expired and the eventful story of the attempt to establish a Church–State system of licensing books in England which stretched back to the days of Henry VIII came to an end. On the whole it was unsuccessful and this is all the more remarkable when the savagery of the methods used to enforce licensing at different periods is considered.

The expiration of the Licensing Act did not mean that book publication and the press were to be free. Licensing was allowed to lapse because it was generally agreed that the system was unworkable. As a means of control the government relied on an expanded libel law. The development of this branch of the law is a fascinating one to trace, but since the Church, save in the case of blasphemous libel, was not directly concerned, it would be out of place to discuss it here. The offence of blasphemous libel lasted into the twentieth century but has now fallen into desuetude. From the end of the seventeenth century, the Church in England no longer attempted to censor books but limited itself to indirect action. During the eighteenth century the Church was inactive, but towards the end of the century the spread of Methodism and the Evangelical revival led to a change of heart. Manners were reformed and eventually in 1802 the Society for the Suppression of Vice was founded. John Bowdler was an original subscriber. At first the Society was confined to London, but it soon spread to other cities, and branches were set up among other places at Bath, Hull and York. The Society had a variety of purposes. It was to prevent the profanation of the Lord's Day, prosecute blasphemy and suppress blasphemous publications, bring the trade in obscene books to a halt, close disorderly houses and suppress fortune tellers. These activities did not go unchallenged. Many felt that the Society was nothing better than a group of busybodies interfering in matters which were not its concern. Sydney Smith dubbed it 'a society for suppressing the vices of those whose incomes do not exceed £500' p.a. Most of the Society's unpopularity was incurred by its campaign of prosecutions for blasphemy which was waged most thoroughly between 1819 and 1823. Its efforts against obscene books on the whole commanded support. Between 1802 and 1807 thirty to forty prosecutions were brought and convictions recorded in every case. Vigilance was relaxed and the tide of pornography rose again, only to be turned back again by a vigorous series of prosecutions between 1817 and 1825. Besides enforcing the existing law by bringing prosecutions, the Society made its provisions widely known by special legal publications. In 1810 *An abstract of the Laws against vice and morality* was published, and by 1832 *The Constable's Assistant*, a compendium of the powers and duties of police officers, had reached four editions. The Society's influence waned and eventually it went out of existence, but it was succeeded by other societies. It was through the medium of such organisations that the Church through the nineteenth century tried to influence publishing in England. The contemporary equivalent of the Society for the Suppression of Vice is the Public Morality Council, which was founded in 1899. It is made up of representatives from all denominations under the presidency of the Bishop of London. From time to time it conducts campaigns against obscene and pornographic books and makes recommendations to the Director of Public Prosecutions. Whether it exercises any widespread influence today is open to doubt.

In the United States the system of licensing books never succeeded in gaining a foothold. The rigid separation of Church and state laid down by the United States constitution also meant that no Church could play an official role in the suppression of books. Ecclesiastical efforts to control books in the United States have by the nature of the constitution to be indirect and are confined to encouraging adherents to enforce existing laws against obscene books or to securing the passage of new legislation. In the nineteenth century the lead in this agitation was taken by the non-conformist Protestant Churches. Today this role—without any saving sense of irony—is taken by the Roman Catholic Church. There were few prosecutions for obscenity in the United States in the early part of the nineteenth century, but after the civil war a puritan reaction took place against the general profligacy and laxity of moral standards. It was against this background that Anthony Comstock, a Protestant zealot, began his forty year campaign for decent literature under the slogan 'Morals, Not Art or Literature'. In 1842 importation of obscene matter was forbidden and further amending legislation was passed in 1857. In 1865 Congress forbade the use of the mails for despatching obscene goods and at the instigation of Comstock comprehensive legislation was passed in 1873. These are the only statutory federal obscene offences. Every state, however, at this period had its local Comstocks and legislation or ordinances were passed in all of them against obscene books. Until the first World War the Protestant Churches were active in enforcing these statutes, but after the war their interest declined and after a short period their place was taken by the Roman Catholic Church.

Today the most active unofficial body in the United States enforcing the obscene literature statutes is the National Organisation for Decent Literature, founded by the Catholic hierarchy in 1938. Its purpose was 'to devise a plan for organising a systematic campaign in all dioceses of the United States against the publication and sale of lewd magazine and brochure literature'. The N.O.D.L. pursues its aim by the following activities: (1) arousing public opinion against objectionable magazines, comics and paperbacked books; (2) more rigorous enforcement of existing law controlling obscene literature; (3) promotion of stricter legislation to suppress obscenity; (4) the preparation of a monthly list of publications disapproved of by the organisation; and (5) the visiting of news-stands and stores to persuade the owners to remove objectionable literature. Since the Organisation can work through diocesan machinery in every part of the United States, its campaign has been effective and has met with considerable success. At the present time it is continuing, but has been the subject of some bitter attacks and has been strongly opposed by the Civil Liberties Union.

This controversy led to the formulation of certain principles to govern the activities of such groups by Mr Vernon Bourke, a Catholic philosopher, and Fr John Courtney Murray, a Jesuit Theologian. They have listed four rules which they consider applicable:

1. Each minority group has the right to censor for its own members, if it so chooses, the contents of the various media of communication, and to protect them, by means of its own choosing, from materials considered harmful according to its standards.

2. No minority group has the right to demand that government should impose a general censorship on material judged to be harmful according to the special standards held within one group.

3. Any minority group has the right to work towards the elevation of standards of public morality . . . through the use of the methods of persuasion and pacific argument.

4. No minority group has the right to impose its own religious or moral views on other groups, through the use of methods of force, coercion or violence.

The Roman Catholic Church still retains its system of censorship, which is applicable only to its own members. The Index system is divided into three parts: the Congregation of the Index; the rules or legislation contained in the code of canon law; and the list of prohibited books, last issued in 1948. Canon law provides *inter alia* the following rules:

1. No Roman Catholic priest or layman may publish any book without prior ecclesiastical approval if it deals with scripture, theology, canon law, etc. (canon 1385).

2. Certain books and classes of books are automatically prohibited by canon law. These include heretical and schismatical books, books supporting

divorce, duelling, suicide, or which evoke spirits, advocate magic, etc. In particular books which 'professedly treat of impure and obscene subjects, narrate or teach them' are forbidden (canon 1399).

3. Permission to read individual banned books may be given local bishops if there is an urgent need to read the book (canon 1402).

Among books included in the 'Index Librorum Prohibitorum' are all the novels of Balzac and Dumas, all the works of Anatole France, J. S. Mill's *Principles of Political Economy*, Pascale's *Pensées*, Richardson's *Pamela*, and John Wilkins's *Discovery of a new world or a discourse tending to prove that 'tis probable there may be another habitable world in the moon, with a discourse concerning the possibility of a passage thither* (1701). Books are added to this Index from time to time. For instance in May 1952 the novels of Alberto Moravia were added to the list. Recently there has been some speculation about its possible reform. Roman Catholics in some countries, notably in Ireland and the United States, seem to treat it more seriously than Roman Catholics in others.

ERNEST VAN DEN HAAG

Quia Ineptum

WHEN *Rigoletto* was first to be performed—in Venice, then under Austrian administration—the censor objected because Victor Hugo's *Le Roi s'amuse*, which Verdi used as his libretto, depicts a king as libertine. *Rigoletto* could not be broadcast today in the United States either except that it is now a classic (and usually sung in Italian): crime pays; love doesn't; virtue is successfully sold down the river . . . it definitely won't do for TV.

We have come a long way since Verdi's time. Has it been progress? Do we have less censorship, in relevant respects, or more? Or do we have different kinds of censorship with different emphases, origins and purposes? Which way is progress? Has there been any?

With rare exceptions, artists and intellectuals object to all censorship: it interferes with their work, with new sentiments, sensibilities, visions, ideas and tropes. Yet many of their arguments against censorship are defective, not to say silly. One argument, attributed to Mayor Jimmy Walker, is: 'no girl has ever been corrupted by a book.'[1] New York's prohibition mayor was not over-familiar with books, of course. His argument is often paraphrased by more literate people though. Yet it implies that literature is uninfluential and therefore harmless—a defence worse than any attack. It is also wrong.

The thoughts and feelings which literature articulates and produces are quite influential; they generate, as well as reflect, and transmit attitudes, ideas and ideals; ultimately they influence conduct, more perhaps than anything else. Shelley rightly spoke of the poets as 'unacknowledged legislators of the world'.[2] The trouble is that the effects of their 'legislation' are hard to foresee—hence it is hard to direct or even to restrain it. Yet in more than one sense, literature

---

[1] Dante already made Francesca testify that books can help: '*Galeotto fu il libro e chi lo scrisse* . . .' Flaubert also suggest the influence of trashy novels on Mme Bovary.

[2] A few qualifications are in order: (1) poets need have no influence even if poems do, (2) poems influence power and authority but embody neither, (3) literature influences dispositions which themselves permit or generate acts, (4) its influence (let alone the acts it influences) is unpredictable as to time, form, effect and effectiveness, and (5) it is hard to predict which books will have effects. Many of these qualifications hold for most 'historical causes'. But the last two make it very hard for a censor to foresee what will have, e.g., 'corrupting' effects and what will not.

reveals and even creates good and evil; books are certainly nearest to the fruits which make us wise and which in any Eden would be forbidden altogether; they influence, they create and they change value discrimination. Thus, they can be helpful or harmful to any existing pattern of social organisation and control, and to the culture of which it is part. That society should recognise this and try to restrain, if not to direct, literature is hardly surprising.

But we do not live—and those of us who are liberals would not want to—in the autocratic regime that is Eden. Moreover, few autocrats have the virtues attributed to God. For the liberal, finally, society is not the God-like custodian of individuals, but only of their liberty:[1] social action is legitimate only where people must be restrained from imposing their will on others, or where, owing to indivisibilities, collective action is required. Thus, no action of competent and consenting persons should be legally restrained unless it can be shown to affect non-consenting persons, or persons incapable of giving legal consent, i.e., to be coercive.

Of course, someone may read a book—presumably a deliberate, voluntary, individual act not in itself harmful to others, and therefore not to be legally restrained—which may affect his behaviour towards me in harmful ways to which I would not consent. Yet, if the principle of liberty is to distinguish between actions the law can, and others it cannot restrain, then, possibly, the acts prompted by it, but not the reading of the book can be restrained. Censorship is excluded. In a sense, all things influence all others. However, the liberal assumption is that individuals are responsible—*eo ipso* capable—of withstanding influences, as distinguished from coercions, that may lead to unlawful acts. Hence the acts, but not the influences—except where there is a clear and present danger that they will bring about unlawful acts—can be legally restrained.

Literature then (and by extension all media of communication and art[2]) should not be restrained except where a 'clear and present' danger to non-consenting persons can be shown. However the danger is

[1] Most liberals do not practise this principle or uphold its practice. But many cling to the theory.

[2] I shall focus on books. Because of relative ease of individual access to both production and consumption, they present a paradigmatic case: censorship of books would always be restrictive. TV and radio are more complex: (1) channels are publicly owned; (2) their number is limited; hence, allowing them to be controlled by the concessionnaires might well reduce the range of liberty unduly. Government intervention here may enlarge as well as restrict freedom and variety. But I have chosen to limit the scope of this essay to the restrictive aspects of censorship.

hardly ever 'clear' and seldom 'present'. *Mein Kampf* could not be legally interdicted by the Weimar Republic: readers might have reacted in less positive ways than they did. Perhaps this should make us suspect the extreme version of the principle of liberty: it helped slaughter too many people.

Jefferson in justifying the principle of liberty was convinced that truth would prevail over error; James Stuart Mill advocated the same principle thinking that truth may not prevail over censorship but was likely to emerge from free discussions. Neither proposition is very meaningful: one may say that error will prevail over truth and be as right. The difficulty is that we are given no criteria for 'prevail'. When, how often, for how long, must acceptance of 'truth' (or 'error') occur to be said to prevail? how influential must it be? And how—apart from acceptance—do we determine which is 'truth' or 'error'? Certainly the argument is bad; if the conclusion is to be upheld, it must rest on other grounds. Either the principle of liberty must be regarded as a sufficient value *per se*, regardless of effects on the prevalence of 'truth'; or it must be assumed that alternative principles would be no more likely to make 'truth prevail', and this prevalence must be thought to be decisive. On the other hand, objections to the principle can be either axiomatic—as the principle is—or sociological, i.e., showing that a different principle is no less likely to lead to desiderata such as 'truth'.

I believe there is another sociological objection quite sufficient to reject the extreme version of the principle of liberty. This sociological hypothesis also explains why no society has ever practised the Jeffersonian principle.[1] A society functions only if its members share a common body of values, and back of it, a common ethos. This permits some divergences but also requires the society, if it is to remain viable, to protect the essential shared values. If this proposition is correct, as I believe, then Jefferson's society—which protects coercively only freedom, allowing people to make any use of it they want (to pursue and cultivate any values) as long as it does not interfere with the freedom of others—is an ideal that cannot be practised.[2] Every society has the right and even the duty to cultivate its ethos, and to protect it from destruction. The ethos may permit liberties—but not to the extent of

---

[1] The principle was held in some form by most philosophers of the enlightenment and is clearly found in Kant.

[2] Thus in the United States, from Jefferson's time to ours, the law has protected values unconnected with freedom, by prohibiting, e.g., Sunday work, drinking, homosexuality, prostitution, gambling, polygamy, etc.

endangering it. Certainly the right of censorship is implied. Within limits, freedom may be part of the ethos. But the ethos must include values beyond the mere universal distribution of the ability to choose (freedom), and these must be protected. Hitherto the means of protection have always included coercion.

The facts discovered by anthropologists, though usually trotted out in arguments about censorship, are quite irrelevant here. Of course there is always some Indian tribe which regards what we consider 'bad' or 'obscene' as 'good' and what we think worthy 'bad' or 'obscene'. This shows that different beliefs are held and that each society has a different ethos—not that each society may not defend the beliefs it holds and the ethos behind it. On the contrary, it suggests the need for such a defence. Nor, of course, does our knowing that different beliefs are held in different cultures imply that one belief is as good (or true) as the other; or that none, or all are true or must be so regarded. There is no common, universal, inter-cultural measure— needed to establish equal or unequal validity or invalidity. And if we use any non-universal intra-cultural measure, beliefs differ in validity according to the standard used. At any rate, in terms of social efficacy, it is not necessary at all that beliefs be true or be demonstrably so. It is enough that they be held and that the holding of some such beliefs is needed for the moral solidarity of any society. Incidentally, historians can show, and somewhat more relevantly, the existence of different beliefs in different periods of the same society. The preference for anthropologists, and their own primitive preferences in these arguments, is a matter of fashion, ultimately a hangover from the Rousseauvean binge.

To defend its values, the rulers of any society must have the right to censor literature then. Granted as much, should they exercise it? Is censorship a necessary and an effective instrument for the protection of the ethos? or, at least more effective and less damaging than the alternatives, including uncensored arts?

The effects of censorship are very hard to evaluate. Certainly it would be a mistake to give much weight to books, movies, etc., actually censored, rightly or wrongly, effectively or ineffectively. The major effect of censorship is not, and is not intended to be, the fate of the few books, movies, etc., to which the censor actually objects. The significant effect is on books that publishers won't publish, and authors won't write, or even conceive, knowing that they could not be printed. Yet, how significant, or how necessary this deterrent function of censorship is we will never know precisely.

On the other hand, it seems fairly likely that, to put it paradoxically, if there were less (formal) censorship, there would be more (informal) censorship. If its values are not defended by formal governmental agencies, society tends to defend them informally. The actual choice is not for or against censorship, but for one form or another. In the United States, for instance, mass media have imposed censorship codes and administrators on themselves in an attempt to forestall, on the one hand, legal censorship, and on the other, pressures, including boycotts, amounting to censorship by various interested groups.

I think the mass media managers estimated the danger correctly and, on the whole, avoided it by their self-imposed censorship. Since in the United States, government censorship would probably be more influenced by capricious, fanatic and incompatible pressure groups than the self-imposed censorship is, the mass media are probably better off this way. Certainly they would be worst off if there were no official or informal attempt to work out standards of censorship: the boycotts and pressures by various interest groups would make mass media far more insipid than they already are.

Having drawn attention to the fact, familiar in jurisprudence (particularly with regard to penal law), that a harsh official act often functions to ward off even harsher and more capricious extra-legal acts aimed at achieving what the legal act aims at, I wish now to consider some of the difficulties of censorship specific to our time. These are two.

First, we live in a pluralistic, untraditional and rapidly changing society; second—and this aggravates the first difficulty—we live in an egalitarian society. The first difficulty makes the censor uncertain as to what values he is defending and society uncertain as to who should censor whom: there is no consensus unless it be so vague that it provides little guidance. There is no established Church, dogma or elite that is informed by and forms prevailing values.[1] Hence, censorship can only defend—fitfully at best—the values precariously, partially and temporarily prevailing in the beliefs of the segment of society thought to be the bearer of its values. A messy business at best. Further, in a well stratified society, even if it be pluralistic, it is easily possible to permit different ways of life to be elaborated within the various strata

[1] Wordsworth already complained (England 1802): . . . no value paramount, no code
No master spirit, no determined road . . .

and groups. Thus a heterodox view, a bold sentiment, an unconventional situation, could be presented to sensibilities that were relied on to sift the acceptable from the unacceptable influences, who, embodying themselves the ethos, were not likely to destroy it. Or, different values could be cultivated in different subcultures which do not communicate much with each other. Switzerland illustrates this possibility. However, in a society which is both mobile and egalitarian and makes profuse use of mass media, one cannot rely on a work of art or philosophy communicating what it was meant to communicate—and might—to just the group it was meant to address.

Still, even in an egalitarian society, communication is stratified via the media: in the United States, by and large, it is possible to say in books what one may not say on stage; on stage what one may not say in movies (or slick magazines); in movies what one may not say on TV. But the media stratification is not rigid. Perhaps it should be. And it might be fostered within book publishing, where, at present, the mass editions stress the most censorable books, at least with regard to sex and violence.[1] Formal or informal measures making paperback books more selective than hardbound ones seem desirable. A person willing to spend an appreciable amount of money on a book is more likely to want it specifically than one who is not. The former person could not easily be prevented—if that were desirable—from gaining access to the work he wants. However, the purchaser of the paperback may indifferently intend to while away an idle hour, and find himself exposed to an undesirable influence which was also undesired. I should much favour a sifting of books before mass editions are printed. But I doubt the possibility—wherefore I am not fully elaborating this approach or the argument for it.[2] As it is, the politically and philosophically heterodox is unlikely to be published in cheap editions anyway: there is no mass market for it. There is a mass market, however, for the literature of sex and violence.

It is on these that controversy and censorship focus. There are two basic questions involved: should society censor any representation of

[1] Perhaps if more people become entirely glued to TV sets, book authors might be given untrammelled freedom.

[2] Still, let me suggest that the matter can be handled without relating it directly to price. For instance, a book printed in 1000 copies may be uncensored. For editions of 1001–10,000, only the grossest 'violations', whatever that may be might be objected to. And for editions from 10,000 up, censorship might be comparatively heavy. Again, our egalitarian ideology would prevent any *formal* move in this direction.

sex or violence in works of art and literature? If so, how are we to discriminate between the permitted and the censorable representations? i.e. what kind of damage are we trying to avoid by means of censorship?

It may be in order briefly to stress once more that communications and representations can have effects, desired or undesired, desirable or undesirable. Thus, the view that to the pure everything is pure, that obscenity is always the projection of the viewer or reader is surely mistaken. Though perceived subjectively, it is a quality of the object that is perceived, just as, for that matter, aesthetic merit is. In both cases the evaluation and effect differ among observers. But that is true for many objective qualities. Difficulties of demonstration must not be confused with non-objectivity—even though they be of great practical moment in reaching consensus.

Now, three kinds of things may be classified as obscene: (1) the suggestion or argument in favour of heterodox attitudes about sexual matters; (2) the stimulation of sexual experience, vicarious or not, or of the desire for it in the 'ordinary' reader or viewer, intended or unintended; (3) the stimulation of the experience of perverse (infantile) forms of sexual satisfaction, vicarious or not, and of the desire for it. About the same classification applies to violence (which may often be included in class three).

These three classes of obscenity may occur in works with or without aesthetic merit. When there is aesthetic merit, one must decide whether it outweighs, or offsets—or, possibly, reinforces—the obscene effects. The obscene effects of the first class are likely to be reinforced by aesthetic merit: though it is not always so, a work of merit is likely to be intellectually more influential than one that is not. Thus if certain intellectual views on sex are to be censored, Shaw, Ibsen, André Gide, or D. H. Lawrence should be regarded as more dangerous than untalented scribblers propagating the same views. However, few people are interested in censoring this kind of obscenity; the issue now has mainly historical importance. In democratic countries, today's censor does not seem to regard intellectual deviation, or argument for it, as influential enough to merit his attention. Or, perhaps as too hard to censor for the reasons suggested above—which explain generally why political and ideological censorship is neglected, but not why obscenity is still censored.

The role of aesthetic merit in the second and third class of obscenity is more doubtful. Some aestheticians (e.g., Santayana[1]) maintain that the work of art does not provide an experience of its subject so much as the experience of its contemplation—an experience held to be, if not an aphrodisiac, at least not itself stirring to the senses. Certainly, the aesthetic experience is the experience of an image, and the contemplation of its perfections may well, as Santayana says, 'cancel lust'. But must it? Even the most tutored sensibility may—however much captivated by the image as such—associate it, *nolente volente*, with its subject, or allow it to stir the senses in some other way. *Amor intellectualis* is not separated always from *amor corporalis* and certainly does not exclude it altogether.

To be sure, the ultra-aesthetic effect depends somewhat on the subject. A still-life of fruit and meat is less likely to stir hunger than a nude is to stir sexual appetites. Perhaps fewer people are hungry, and less fundamentally so, than are sexually frustrated; and erotic appetites seem less definitely satisfiable.[2] There is no doubt in my mind that the artistically most perfect representation of sexual matters may quicken sexual appetites in the most perfect observer. And it certainly can do so in less than perfect observers. However, aesthetic merit here is likely, if not to eliminate, to reduce rather than augment the obscene, effect. The pin-up has it all over art, if it comes to sheer erotic stimulation. In this respect, obscenity as sexual heterodoxy, intellectually argued (1) differs from obscenity as sensual stimulation (2 and 3).

Thus, one question is whether because of this and because of its general desirability, aesthetic merit suffices to let the work go uncensored despite the remaining likely 'obscene' effects. However, aesthetic merit is no less hard to demonstrate than obscene effect is—and it is only marginally relevant to 'obscenity': at most it diminishes the impact of the subject on the senses. Thus, the efforts made in English courts, to establish the literary merits of *Lady Chatterley's Lover*, and in American courts to establish those of *Ulysses*, seem misplaced or at least uneconomic. Both works might well go uncensored regardless of aesthetic merit. *Lady Chatterley's Lover* preaches a heterodox

---

[1] Quite apart from its merit, his view seems more characteristic of Santayana's rationalistic temperament and attitude towards art and life than of art and life. (His might profitably be compared with Sir Kenneth Clark's view.)

[2] Perhaps they are more easily kindled by communications, in our culture, owing to the fact that the representation of sexual matters is not as permitted as the representation of non-sexual ones. Finally, the visual is, *per se*, part of the erotic, whereas visual aspects are not so much linked to the gastronomic.

morality but can hardly be considered sensually stimulating.[1] And to read *Ulysses* for erotic stimulation surely is to go about it in so circuitous and difficult a way as to deserve a reward for bravery. Thus, both these books might go uncensored—regardless of their merits—because of the sheer unlikeliness, owing to their style and total content, that anyone will read them for the sake of erotic stimulation, or be gratified if he does.

Aside from the question of artistic merit, and granted that, in principle, we can define what is obscene or censorable, practical application still remains cloudy. The denotative meaning of what has been connotatively agreed on will always be doubtful, to say the least. One may wonder whether a sexual description is bereft of obscenity when it arises from novelistic context, though, isolated it is deemed obscene. Certainly placement plays an important role: dirt is misplaced matter.[2] But in either case, the description can be arousing. (I think that contextual meaningfulness is more important in the case of violence, simply because it is more undesirable that violence be presented as valuable *per se* than that sex be.) What will be so is, in the nature of the matter, a fairly arbitrary decision.

If the standard of obscenity is sociologically well founded (a hard thing to imagine), if by 'censorable' we mean that which the majority wants censored, there is an obvious difficulty. If art were censored whenever it deals with the non-accepted—whenever it presents relevant new perceptions, visions or values—perhaps with the intent, or effect of making them acceptable, we would run the danger of denying the innovatory role that literature and art necessarily play. In short, we would censor art out of existence. Yet any other standard would of necessity revert to some sort of dogmatically enshrined or interpreted values which, as mentioned above, is impractical in our society. To this dilemma I have no real solution. It is part of the permanent

---

[1] I do not wish to forgo the occasion for saying that I think *Lady Chatterley's Lover* is a didactic, dull and often silly book preaching a sophomorically para-Nietzschean morality. I marvel at the serious critics who testified otherwise and wonder whether their principle of freedom has not corrupted them as much as others were corrupted by their need to suppress it. Generally one might reflect whether principles—even good ones—are not as often corruptive of truth and decency as sordid lucre is reputed to be. Anything, it seems, when heedlessly pursued, may corrupt both judgment and honesty.

[2] 'Obscene' most probably comes from 'caenum' (dirt), possibly from obscaenum (freely translated: inappropriate, improper, ugly) certainly not, as often thought, from 'obscurum' (dark, hidden) Abraham Kaplan's excellent 'Obscenity as an Aesthetic Category' (*Law and Social Problems*, autumn 1955) notwithstanding. I have learned from, but cannot altogether follow Kaplan's taxonomy, mainly because it includes elements of evaluation which I prefer to offer independently.

tension and compromise between renewal and conservation which characterises our society more than others. However, this part is not very important in our society because it is confined to one area: sex (and possibly violence). Let us see how it is dealt with.

In the United States, a major part of the dilemma is not so much solved as thrust aside: not enough influence is ascribed to heterodox ideas *as such* to bother censoring their publication.[1] One may fearlessly argue for anything political, moral or even sexual as long as one presents only an intellectual argument. Textbooks for primary and secondary schools, and occasionally books for public libraries are the exception to this rule. (Efforts to bring pressure on college reading selections have been too unsuccessful to warrant consideration.) Since it may be suspected that many children never will read books beyond those assigned in school—if these—the concern with texts is not unreasonable. Our mystical belief in the efficacy of education, and its para-religious moral function may further intensify the nearly obsessive zeal with which school books sometimes are sifted.

There often is pressure on the boards which decide on textbooks and indirectly on publishers and authors. And sometimes there is a similar pressure on librarians in public libraries. But pressure to prevent books from being made obligatory reading (in schools) or from being made available free of charge (in schools and libraries), however wise or silly, however effective or unsuccessful, cannot be defined as censorship. It does not even have analogous effects: school children or library users remain quite free to read any books they wish on their own.[2] Censorship prohibits or prevents publication, sale or showing of what is censored, and makes it unavailable. Both schools and libraries must always be selective; libraries mainly for financial reasons, schools also for didactic reasons. Their selectivity—however biased or influenced—never amounts to censorship: to have to pay reasonable and customary prices to get a book or see a movie cannot be called censorship.

Censorship, in the proper sense of the word, is now applied only when works are believed to be sexually stimulating to a degree, or by means, judged excessive—i.e., obscene, lewd, lascivious or indecent—and capable of 'corrupting' ordinary persons. With regard to violence, too, contagious effects are feared, though censorship is more

[1] There also is the Jeffersonian tradition referred to previously.
[2] Purchase prices are not likely to be a serious obstacle for serious readers today.

often advocated than actually applied. That the standard of 'obscenity' cannot be so vague as to make most action less predictable than is usual has been explained. Yet, however distressing to lawyers, vagueness does not greatly interfere with the social function of censorship.

Prima facie, this social function is puzzling. After all, sexual activity is not itself contrary to the prevailing ethos. Why should it be prohibited then to arouse the desire for it, or to stimulate it, or to satisfy the desire for it vicariously? (Perversion seems more likely to be censored *qua* sexual than *qua* perverse.) Certainly relics of the originally anti-sexual Judeo-Christian tradition have been preserved; and official acts often are guided by moralities which have disappeared in practice since, in such matters, there usually is a 'cultural lag'. Yet this explanation, though helpful, seems insufficient. The 'lag' in this area itself requires explanation as does the tradition we cling to. And the Christian tradition has officially been abolished—e.g., in the Soviet Union; in some places it never meant much—e.g., in Asia; and yet there is censorship directed against sexual stimulation in these places. Finally, the cultural lag concept hardly explains the censors' disregard of intellectual heterodoxy in sex matters; traditionally harsher measures were taken against it than against mere pornography.

The very vigour with which censorship in sexual matters is contested from both sides suggests that it is more than a lifeless historical relict, that the explanation lies deeper. In all societies some things are tabooed. They are not the same things, but taboos always include some sexual activities, and, particularly, incestuous and regressively infantile ones. Sometimes taboos are placed on acts; no less often on things symbolising these acts, or associated with them, or deemed capable of arousing desire for them. Indeed, many apparently non-sexual taboos may be explained in terms of the sexual association with the tabooed activity.

As Freud has pointed out, what is tabooed is usually something that is, or at some level of development was, strongly, if perhaps unconsciously desired. The desire is felt to be dangerous by the person who, in the course of his development, has repressed it; and by society for the same reason; and also because society rests to some extent on such desires not being reawakened.[1] The danger signal, which indicates that the repressed desires may be rearoused, is anxiety. It is to avoid anxiety that the tabooed is avoided, and, in the first place tabooed. Anxiety may be felt in the presence of what is associated with repressed

---

[1] At least not in the form in which they arose and with which they may remain associated in fantasy.

infantile stages of development (as noted the etymology of 'obscene' seems to allude to the anal stage); and also if strong non-perverse sexual stimuli occur when no physical contact permitting a release of tension is immediately available. Such stimuli may recall masturbation fantasies and the masturbatory stage of development. Strong libidinal stimuli without sexual relations thus may mobilise the defences, the ego originally built when weak and in danger of being swamped by the demands of the id in their direct libidinal form. Finally, the fantasy stimulation of sexual desire often leads back to stages of development in which sex and violence were identified or closely related (wherefore, indeed, one does sometimes combine with, sometimes take the place of, the other in both fantasy and reality.) In short, the adult ego feels personality integration—its own control—threatened by stimuli that were originally handled through repression; it reacts with anxiety, and with a tendency to ward off the threat by reconstructing the original defence which was, after all, a form of censorship.

As Freud stressed, taboos, however severe, usually are ambivalent. On occasion the prohibited act can be performed, actually or symbolically. Or, the taboo interdicts actions associated with the prohibited act, marginally or symbolically, but ignores the act itself. Sometimes the letter is observed, the better to defeat the spirit, or meaning of the prohibition. Taboos function as obsessive symptoms in a neurosis often do. Indeed, obsessive neuroses have been characterised as travesties of religion. Often the superego seems content—and the anxiety level does not rise—if the taboo is observed ritualistically, if the symbol, rather than that which it symbolises, is banned. This is a way of repudiating and all the same indulging the tabooed act—of giving both the id and the superego its due.[1]

I believe that the explanation, if not the justification, of censorship lies here: it is a compromise—with all the characteristic obsessive displacement and ambivalence—between the original wish to indulge infantile, anal, oral, and ultimately all sexual desires, and the later wish to control them. The difficulties the ego experiences in attempting to settle the conflict between id and superego are resolved, or 'acted out', in the ineffectual but anxiety-reducing control of symbols that we call censorship.[2]

---

[1] The technique of doing so utilises the infantile identification of symbol with act.

[2] Let me call attention once more to the etymology of 'obscene' (Fn. p. 119). The anxiety arousing quality of repressed anal desires related to dirt (i.e., excrement) is well established in psychoanalytic theory.

Censorship serves both to curb and to stimulate, to intensify desire while restraining it. Above all, it reduces anxiety. Its role is similar to that of fashion in clothing. It veils some things, thereby investing the hidden with more attention, protecting it and the viewer and adding to the desire for (and impact of) the unveiling.[1] Like censorship, fashion can make allusions meaningful and more interesting even than the naked truth. In the nature of the matter, then, censorship is likely to be capricious and inconsistent, as fashion is. What lawyers must regard as the censors' ineptness is an inherent characteristic.

I have offered some hypotheses, to justify censorship in principle and to explain its origin, function and effects, as well as its peculiar ambivalence. Let me conclude with a few tangential considerations.

Granted that censorship functions to reduce anxiety, is this always necessary? Would Medusa's head threaten them less if people were less 'neurotic'? Perhaps. But I know of no culture without taboos. There are many even in the most primitive cultures. (I should be unwilling anyway to give up civilisation for so paltry a gain as the absence of taboos.) Individual evidence seems to confirm what social evidence suggests: I have not found that well-analysed people, including psychoanalysts, lack repressions, obsessions, rituals, etc. Often these are fairly economic ways of managing a problem. They seem to be part of the human predicament rather than specific and avoidable difficulties of our civilisation. This is to say that the sort of problem, and the kind of provision made for it are permanent; it is not to say that a particular organisation or degree of censorship are.

By and large, the *status quo* seems fairly satisfactory to me. The uncertainty as to what censors and ultimately courts, will find 'obscene' is unavoidable, does little harm, and has its uses: we may call it flexibility or responsiveness. Not much is lost, I think, by almost any conceivable censorship of sex in TV or movies. (Nor is such censorship contagious.) As for movies, it may help if children were not permitted access to those meant for adults except with written permission of their guardians. (The alternative is to treat the whole audience as though it consisted of children.)

There is one change which I have advocated in the past and want to advocate again. I should prohibit printing anything about the sexual

---

[1] I owe the analogy with fashion to Eric Larrabee's urbane and enlightening 'The Cultural Context of Sex Censorship' (*Law and Contemporary Problems*, autumn, 1955).

life of any identifiable living person without his consent. The advantage would be twofold: primarily privacy would be protected; and secondarily titillation of a particularly repulsive sort that requires fantasies to be attached to names and to be 'factual' would be reduced. I can see no harm to any actual public interest.[1] Perhaps the sale of newspapers and magazines would be reduced. I shouldn't regret that.

I am reiterating this proposal not because I hope that it will be adopted now, but because it suggests that the reader interested in sexual stimulation need do no more than look at the newspapers. The censorship of obscenity in art and fiction must be regarded as a ceremonial rearguard action. To battle against it, however, seems to me to engage in behaviour even more quixotic than that of the censors.

---

[1] Factual reporting on court proceedings must be excepted, of course.

MAURICE GIRODIAS

More Heat Than Light

To the memory of Kinsey, son of Voltaire

'TO deprave and corrupt' is my business. It is my business to publish those forbidden books, those outrageous obscenities which are being discussed here. I have been invited to participate in this collective study because of my specialised experience of libertine literature; and I feel that I can only express my appreciation of this invitation by being entirely candid in what I have to say.

It is not always comfortable to sit on so many taboos at one time; some kick you and others keep melting away. I have been indicted, prosecuted, sentenced, threatened, insulted and aggressed so often and in such different manners because of the books I publish, that I have developed a philosophy of my own.

I have been wondering for many years at the uncontrolled violence of those reactions, at the intensity of the prejudice. Reading is a private affair; whoever decides to read a book invests a certain sum of intelligence and imagination in that enterprise, which is required to understand the author's intention and reconstruct the fiction he has created. Reading, therefore, is a positive activity, which must be carefully distinguished from such pastimes as seeing a film, for instance, which requires only receptivity. Whoever reads a book—whatever the book may be—must therefore be endowed with a certain freedom of choice, with an ability to judge and criticise, which places that person on a certain mental level.

Why, then, must society (represented by private associations, the clergy, and a number of government officials) exert a *moral censorship* on the reader's preferences or habits?

If one goes a little deeper into the problem, one soon discovers that moral censorship is in fact only exerted on sexual themes. G. Legman remarked that one is allowed to read about the most horrible crimes, which are against nature, while being forbidden to read about sex, which is the very expression of nature.

This discrepancy sheds a rather revealing light on the question of erotic literature. What is important is not that question in itself, but our attitude towards it. Nobody has ever been able to prove that erotic literature is harmful; nobody has ever even tried.

Why, then, are so many people shocked, or terrified, or revolted by that very notion? That, it seems, is the real problem.

In establishing the Olympia Press in 1953, I had three major aims in view. First of all, I had no money and I wanted to make some as fast as possible. Then, I wanted to come back to publishing after a disastrous and heart-rending failure which had occurred a few years before. And finally I wanted to see how far I could go, single-handed, in a deliberate attempt to destroy censorship as a moral institution, as a tradition, as a method of government.

The Olympia Press published, right from the beginning, good books outlawed by Anglo-American censorship, and stark pornography. Perhaps I will be given some credit one day for having introduced to the English-speaking public such writers as Samuel Beckett (*Watt*: 1953; etc.), Jean Genet, Vladimir Nabokov, William Burroughs, de Sade, J. P. Donleavy, Raymond Queneau, and a number of others, of whom some have not yet been 'discovered' by my British and American *confrères*. For this category of authors, at any rate, I feel that in the end I will be pardoned, if not praised. But for the others, for the pornographers, for the authors of such one-sided masterpieces as *Who Pushed Paula*, *White Thighs*, *The Chariot of Flesh*, *The Whip Angels*, and *The Sexual Life of Robinson Crusoe*, for those torrents of bad taste— how can I ever be forgiven?

And yet, I am by no means prepared to disavow them. Are they mercenary writers? Yes, certainly; but then all writers work for money. Further, I refuse to believe that because a book contains obscenities, it is necessarily bad. I hold the view that an anonymous novel, written for money and filled with erotic scenes, can nevertheless be quite acceptable as literature. I need only list my pseudonymous authors: Harriet Daimler, Pauline Réage, Pierre Angélique, Frances Lengel, Akbar del Piombo, Maxwell Kenton, Henry Crannach, Palmiro Vicarion, Faustino Perez, Thomas Peachum, Willy Baron, William Talsman, etc.

It was the fashion, some years ago, to denounce Henry Miller as a corrupt writer who introduced obscenities into his novels in order to make money. Indeed, I have taken great pains on several occasions to convince French police and magistrates that such a supposition was absurd: had Miller really wanted to make a fortune out of pornography, he would have toned down the sex scenes in his books to make them acceptable in the English-speaking countries; or alternatively he would have allowed his books to be reprinted in those countries in expurgated form. By refusing to compromise, he vindicated his sincerity.

This example is significant, because in Miller's case many who accused him of such ulterior motives did so out of professional jealousy. Sex sells a book and the academic novelists introduce as much watered-down and allusive sex into their works as the literary etiquette of the time permits. It is quite obvious that these 'respectable' craftsmen regarded the sudden appearance of Henry Miller—that savage competitor who with his first book disrupted all the accepted rules, and who desecrated all the rosy mysteries with his elephantine onslaughts—as much more of an economic calamity than an aesthetic one. And yet he appeared as the herald of a new artistic era, in which the material to be used by the writer would be himself; his own flesh and blood, sweat and semen—instead of being drawn from the stuff of Victorian Odysseys, dreams of glory, and idylls for schoolgirls. . . .

Sir Alan Herbert, representing the British Society of Authors, expressed quite clearly and honestly such a view in the following declaration made before the Committee on the Obscene Publications Bill: 'When I write a book I do not think: "I am not going to corrupt." I write a book saying: "I must do my love scenes and my sex scenes truthfully and sincerely," taking care, of course, and using artistic restraint, but I certainly do not think whether I am going to corrupt or deprave anybody. The thought never enters my mind or the publisher's. It is the other man you want to get after, the man who sits down and thinks—and in this memorandum I have used a good old English expression, but I am sure you will pardon it—"I want to make my readers as randy as I can, as often as I can." That is the man you are after always. He is not bothering whether he corrupts anybody. He is frankly marketing lust, he is marketing something he knows he can sell. The problem you have to face in clause 2 is to distinguish, shall we say, between myself and the other fellow. . . .'

It may be assumed that Sir Alan is not after Henry Miller—because Henry Miller has gradually been recognised as a sincere artist in the course of the past thirty years, and it would not be fashionable at this stage to condemn him. Sir Alan, however, is certainly after those 'who market lust because it is something they know they can sell . . .' and who do so without using any of the 'artistic restraint' which he finds himself forced to observe. In that context, 'artistic restraint' must

E

naturally be understood in its proper sense as: a form of auto-censorship without which you are not allowed to operate on the middle class market; it is 'artistic' only in the sense that much talent is required to manipulate the correct amount of sex compatible both with good taste, as understood by the middle class, and commercial success.

That natural tendency of the conventional novelists to 'corner the market', and outlaw what they consider as unfair competition, is supported by their attendant cortège of critics and publishers, and constitutes one of the main foundations of censorship.

Is the test of good writing financial integrity? I am afraid that it is purely a question of degree; there are some highly respected masters who possess an unusual sense of business.

As to those pseudonymous authors of mine, may I say that, strange as it may seem, their primary object, at least for the best of them, was not really money. I sincerely believe that they were more attracted by the opportunity of writing a book and by the experience it represented for them, than by the meagre salary they were paid for their work. They were allowed complete freedom of expression, and they seldom took that freedom as an invitation to cheapness. Quite a few of them have now undertaken a 'legitimate' career, and their earlier and clandestine experiences have certainly proved very useful to them in this new phase.

What, then, can be the difference between a 'pornographic' novel and a 'non-pornographic' one?

Technically the problems are identical—style, plot, construction, dialogue, etc. The themes are the same: I suppose that the human passions constitute the theme of at least 95% of the novels which are being published today.

Naturally, quality varies. But in each category there exist parallel scales of value, e.g., you can have a *bad* non-pornographic novel and a *good* pornographic one—the final qualification depending exclusively on the talent and intelligence of the author.

Is the difference one of morality, or of social usefulness? My contention is that conventional novels are no less immoral, or socially harmful, or false, or anything else, than allegedly pornographic novels.

The final difference between the two categories lies only in the scope of language used, rather than anything else: the adoption of taboo words by the one kind of writer, and their exclusion by the other; and even more deeply, in the vivid description of sexual impulses and actions by the one category, and the painstaking circumnavigation of such subjects by the other.

Once again, great variations of quality exist inside of each category, and they must constantly be kept in mind if we do not want to obscure the issue hopelessly—as is currently being done. Between Jean Genet's novel, *Our Lady of the Flowers*, and a brainless obscenity, there is as much difference as between the best works of conventional fiction and a cheap murder story.

When it comes to defining such adjectives as 'obscene' or 'pornographic' as used in relation to books, the promotors of censorship themselves fail to produce anything but further adjectives. For instance, the definitions given by the members of the Select Committee on the Obscene Publications Bill, already mentioned, or the witnesses who appeared before that committee, are simply words like: indecent, shocking, dirty, lewd, filthy, disgusting. No other words are used— simply because there are none.

But why were such adjectives used in place of a clear and intelligible formulation? The Committee's purpose was to elaborate the new British law on obscene publications, and its elementary task was therefore to define obscene publications for the courts.

Instead of that, we have a stream of frightened epithets, which reveal the entirely subjective, emotional attitude of those men who are called to inspire and guide censorship.

The problem of censorship versus eroticism is deep and far-reaching precisely because it affects so many people with such irrational violence.

The reasons given by the advocates of censorship to justify it can be entered in two categories: it is a social necessity, particularly in the field of education; and it answers a moral necessity of a traditional and religious nature.

The argument of 'social necessity' has been stripped to the bone in the past century. But the words of the law remain, and they reveal its deep intentions quite clearly. Writing is obscene, in the sense adopted by the British courts since 1868, when, 'the tendency of the matter charged as obscenity is to deprave and corrupt those whose minds are open to such immoral influences and into whose hands a publication of this sort may fall. . . .'

In other words, the good people, the working classes, must be kept in blissful ignorance of the universal nature of sex, and, above all, of the legitimate nature of eroticism.

The whole thing appears today as such a wretched hypocrisy that nobody would argue in favour of that thesis. It would be difficult indeed to prove that there is a class of individual for whom eroticism is harmful, and another one for whom it is not; nor do we find any more commentators like the English surgeon, Acton, (as reported by Havelock Ellis) who wrote in his treatise on sexual questions, one hundred years ago, that to attribute sexual pleasure to women is 'a vile aspersion'.

However, the argument of social usefulness still survives in a disguised form: even if adults can do what they want, and damn themselves if they choose to, children must be protected 'against evil influences'.

There is something rather baffling in that contention. We are asked to believe that even where moral censorship is no longer applicable to adults, it is still applicable to children; and that the danger of children accidentally or maliciously reading certain erotic books, written especially for the adults, is such that those books should be suppressed, in order to protect the children's purity. And furthermore, that adults should accept this sacrifice as a sacred duty. It is not worthwhile going very deeply into that sort of argument—but its very existence deserves attention as it gives an idea of the intellectual level on which the debate has been situated up to now.

Children are not interested in adult erotic games. They can only be attracted to so-called pornography by the intensely false and secretive attitude of their elders towards that hackneyed mirage. And if those children one day become dull, conventional, and hypnotised by their self-imposed fears, we know very well that pornography, under any form, will have had nothing to do with it; and that the example set by their parents, and the atmosphere of frustration and hypocrisy in which they are brought up, will bear all the responsibility for that fatal outcome.

In spite of the persistence of many reactionary currents, the evolution towards intellectual freedom has been noticeable in the English-speaking countries since the last war. The recent publication of *Lady Chatterley's Lover*, in both England and America, and of *The Tropic of Cancer* in the latter country, are considerable events, and have a great significance—as these two books were considered for many years symbols of outlaw literature.

It will now be a matter of a few years before the evolution is complete and moral censorship discarded once and for all, at least by the Western countries: this is the natural, logical and desirable outcome of the present movement forward.

But, although this prospect is now clearly in view, it is still distant, and we still have occasion to study at close range the censorship phenomenon; thus enabling us to judge what we are experiencing now, in the light of what we may experience in a few years time.

Between man as he is and the moral image he has created of himself there is a gap which cannot easily be filled. Kinsey has given us an elaborate image of what he calls the human animal, and we cannot deny the practical accuracy of his findings. We *are* that average unit which achieves under proper conditions 3·3 orgasms per week; we have so much homosexuality in our make-up, and more masturbation than we would care to admit. We are that chequered hero so completely engulfed by society, and so completely motivated by education and circumstantial pressures, that we do not produce one idea we would dare call our own in a thousand vibrations our brains generate.

We spend an enormous amount of energy in trying to conform to that moral image we have been given of ourselves without ever questioning its validity only because we feel that to create an image of our own would cost us even more energy. We are desperately trying to look like something we are not, and the contortions to which we subject ourselves are enough to explain all the horrors and failures of modern society.

Although the religious sources of censorship are obvious, it is remarkable that many people who pose as complete atheists still instinctively obey the moral code set by the Jewish and Christian traditions; these traditions which are seldom the consequence of an original teaching, but more often the expression of a social structure.

For instance, the sexual morality advocated by the Christian Church rests mostly on St Paul's teachings on asceticism, as expressed in the first epistle to the Corinthians: '. . . I would that all men were even as I myself . . . But every man hath his proper gift of God, one after this manner, and another after that. I say therefore to the unmarried and widowed: It is good for them if they abide even as I. But if they cannot contain, let them marry; for it is better to marry than to burn.'

This epistle has been abundantly commented on before, and interpreted in different ways; it is viewed with some misgivings by the Roman Catholics who do not find in it a corroboration of their views on the sanctity of procreation, in opposition to the infamy of sensual pleasures. Perhaps the reason is to be found in the original destination of that epistle. Paul's message was not meant for a large public, for the population of a city or country; 'the Corinthians' were the members of the 'Church of Corinth' and numbered less than a hundred disciples—ascetics for whom the Revelation was not the definition of a new mode of social behaviour, but a spiritual technique. It was the open door to a dynamic experience requiring a strict discipline and considerable sacrifices . . . but sacrifices which were to be wilfully made, because 'it is better to marry than to burn' and one has to find the ascetic technique best suited to one's 'proper gift of God'.

Whereas the Vedantic and Buddhist religions have retained that dynamic sense of asceticism, the Roman Church has allowed confusion to develop when the clergy started to play a growing social, economic and political role, during the Middle Ages. The Protestant schisms failed to restore the original meaning of the Christian teachings, and their intervention resulted in a complete integration of religion in the social structure.

The rules of behaviour to which we are subjected today—consciously or not—derive from Talmudic and Christian teachings meant for another era, for other peoples, and above all, for a restricted elite obedient to a mystic ideal. Those rules have been transformed in the course of the centuries, to serve the needs of an upper class, and have been incorporated in our laws, in our institutions, in our beliefs. We are required to follow them blindly, never to question their validity, never to wonder about their human utility.

By the practice of confession, the Catholic Church has established its domination on firm ground. A code of conduct has been defined; its divine origin has been proclaimed with hypnotic insistence to generation after generation; a list of horrible spiritual punishments has been edicted to crush the transgressor. The priest alone is to manipulate the threat of punishment; by way of confession he can absolve or condemn, his power over the penitent being practically boundless.

In Protestant countries, that method of guidance has been replaced by a code of very strict ethics, enforced by the means of institutionalised spying—each person being taught from earliest childhood that no 'forbidden' action can be successfully hidden from the thousand eyes of society. Where the Catholics invoke the Virgin Mary, the Protestants invoke Good Taste.

The socio-political function of those religions is particularly visible when one compares certain fundamental rules they have presented as edicts. Sexual freedom, for instance, is strictly banished, and sexual impulses are controlled with maximum severity—although it would be difficult to justify that severity with the help of the early Christian teachings. On the other hand, killing is not only permissible, but a duty if one is called upon to participate in a war. Such deep inconsequence reveals more than anything else the complete subjection of modern religion to short-range political aims.

One would have believed that the Communist Revolution, which fought the religious traditions with such vigour from the start, would have at least attempted to rid the world of the sexual superstitions as well. It is quite remarkable that, after a few inconsequential manifestations in favour of free love, the idea was entirely abandoned, and the Communist countries developed their own brand of puritanism, which seems much worse than the original thing. Moral censorship is for any government, and particularly for authoritarian ones, a very real source of political power—a method of individual and collective control which they have inherited directly from their former religious organisations.

Obviously we cannot call that code of moral conduct, which we are forced to obey by legal and social pressures, a system of 'natural' morals as long as it represents war as sacred and pleasure as illicit.

Perhaps it would not be quite as easy to force half-enlightened people to believe in the old sexual superstitions, if those people, or the majority at any rate, did not find a certain comfort in moral censorship.

Sexual competition has now taken on an aspect which is quite different from what it was in primitive societies. Today, it happens in many cases that the choice of a wife is dictated less by lust or love, than by the requirements of social representation. Problems of precedence, questions of decorum, become much more important than natural satisfaction. To the aged and wealthy husband of a young and charming woman, sex is a half-forgotten function, and he views with much distaste any allusion to its existence, in books, films or anywhere. To the father of a middle-class family, such allusions are even more disturbing; to imagine that his wife may somehow learn that there exist males sexually more attractive, clever, or more enterprising than him, constitutes a threat to his peace of mind. His growing indifference leaves a deep dissatisfaction in him, of a vague and ill-defined nature, and the very notion of a healthy couple making love is something which he finds unbearable—and which he calls indecent, disgusting, filthy, etc.

There may exist other explanations of the censorship phenomenon besides jealousy, fear, frustration and socio-political conservatism disguised under religious motives—but I cannot think of any.

It is true that the human mind is essentially repetitive. Like the organs of the body, it tends to re-enact the same movements always, at the same intervals. It takes centuries, or thousands of years, to eradicate a false idea, or change a tradition.

But today the problem has become suddenly very urgent. We have conquered in a few years such enormous powers that we find ourselves unable to control them. There exists an abysmal distance between our scientific and technical discoveries, and the degree of *human* intelligence of those who operate them. We are sending astronauts to the moon, and we forbid them to read Henry Miller.

The two poles of the human horizon—love and death—have become dramatically obscured. By a strange mechanism of reflexion, our fear of death has been transformed into a belief in the inevitability of war and universal extinction; in that sense, the bomb is more powerful as a symbol of our metaphysical impasse than as a means of destruction. . . . As to love, which set in motion such vast movements as the French Revolution and Marxism, it soon floundered into the Napoleonic conquests and Stalinism.

If we carefully and honestly analyse our beliefs, we will not find one particle of reality among the mental dregs which have accumulated in us from generation to generation since the stone age—since our sea-going ancestors. Such bright words as democracy are empty of any real significance, and only indicate a blurred tendency of our instincts.

We have created a mental world for ourselves in which all the negative and painful elements vastly predominate: fear, responsibility, duty, fatality. Our general attitude towards sex and sexual pleasure is entirely conditioned by our sado-masochistic mental routines.

Obscenity and pornography are ugly phantoms which will disappear in the morning light, when we rehabilitate sex and eroticism. We must accept love and lust as complementary movements, and not as incompatible elements. We must rediscover desire as the source of all the positive actions in our life, and stop opposing every natural instinct and every pleasure-giving activity.

That result cannot be achieved without a series of mental shocks and convulsions. My sincere, if paradoxical wish, is that my activity as a publisher shall have helped to destroy a few taboos, and to clear the air.

WALTER ALLEN

*The Writer and the
Frontiers of Tolerance*

IN 1850, Thackeray wrote a preface to *Pendennis* in which he said:

Even the gentlemen of our age—this is an attempt to describe one of them, no better nor worse than most educated men—even these we cannot show as they are, with the notorious foibles and selfishness of their lives and education. Since the author of *Tom Jones* was buried, no writer of fiction among us has been permitted to depict to his utmost power a MAN. We must drape him, and give him a certain conventional simper. Society will not tolerate the Natural in our Art. . . . You will not hear—it is best to know it—what moves in the real world, what passes in society, in the clubs, colleges, messrooms—what is the life and talk of your sons.

The passage is interesting for several reasons. One is that Thackeray himself was a novelist whose tremendous talent was partly hamstrung by his reluctant acceptance of the official morality of his day. He knew the kind of writer he ought to have been, just as he was aware of the hypocrisy implicit in the Victorian view of sex. He had written in 1840: 'The world does not tolerate now such satire as that of Hogarth and Fielding. But a man who has walked through Regent Street of a night or has been behind the scenes of the Opera, or has even been to a theatre, and looked up to that delectable part of the house, the second tier of the boxes, must know that the *Rake's* and *Harlot's Progress* is still by no means concluded. . . . The same vice exists, only we don't speak about it; the same things are done, but we don't call them by their names.' And he also said: 'If I was to write as I would like, I would adopt the style of Fielding and Smollett; but society would not tolerate it.' He was not a man to challenge the age, but in *Pendennis*, though it is not easy to see it now, he plainly felt he had gone rather far. 'A little more frankness than is customary,' he wrote, 'has been attempted in this story.' And something of his unease at the prudery of his age came through to readers, enough to enable Bagehot to write: 'No one can read Mr Thackeray's writings without feeling that he is perpetually treading as close as he dare to the border line that separates the world that may be described in books from the world which it is prohibited so to describe.'

But Thackeray's preface is interesting for another reason. Addressed to women, who are assured that the author has no intention of lifting for them the veil that hides masculine mystery but that what lies behind the veil is very horrid, it assumes an absolute difference between men and women where feelings about sex—the word is not used—are concerned. It is men, the view seems implicit, who have the prerogative of 'notorious foibles and selfishness'. It is men, even though gentlemen, who cannot be shown as they are. Men, even gentlemen, are very different from what they appear; but women are exactly what they seem. Regretting the passing of the artistic freedom that was Fielding's, it seems never to strike Thackeray that it might be just as much worth doing though, given the temper of the times, no less impossible, for a novelist to depict to his utmost power a WOMAN. Eight years later, Flaubert in France did precisely this in *Madame Bovary* and in consequence had to face a prosecution for offending public morality and religion. He was acquitted, but even so it was not until 1886 that an English translation of his novel was published.

The third reason for our interest in Thackeray's preface is the spectacle of his hankering after a golden age of freedom of expression based on the open recognition of the facts of sexual life, including the human being's 'notorious foibles and selfishness' in sexual matters. Here we must surely sympathise with Thackeray. In most respects, though certainly not in all, our society is vastly more permissive sexually than was Victorian; yet I doubt whether it can truly be said that we are much more at ease with sex than Thackeray and his contemporaries were. We at least admit its existence, and it may even be more of a problem to us than it was to the Victorians. That it is a problem for us is proved, if proof is necessary, by the very solemnity with which we discuss it. After half a million years of man on earth, during which time every single human being has been produced by sexual intercourse, one might have expected that by now sex would present no difficulty; but, as we all know, outside dirty jokes sex is no laughing matter, and in public discussion of the subject a tone of the most righteous high-mindedness is obligatory to all taking part, whatever their point of view, repressive or permissive. Repressives and Permissives alike unite in condemning the constant and all-pervading exploitation of sex that is one of the most striking aspects of the public face of western society. Indeed, there are times when one feels that our old friend the Man from Mars, dropped down in London or New York to visit the theatres and cinemas, travel the escalators in the

Underground, inspect the bookstalls, read the newspapers and magazines and listen to the pop songs, could hardly not conclude that he had been projected into a society whose members were permanently on heat and in which the condition of being on heat was regarded as the highest felicity.

We know more about sex in theory than any generation before us, and perhaps because of this, exist, to borrow a phrase from Robert Graves's poem, in a new confusion of our understanding. We haven't, as yet, reached a new understanding of our confusion; and a sane attitude towards sex, such as is implicit in *The Canterbury Tales*, where sex is seen as a normal, natural human activity, often pleasurable and also often very funny in its by-products, but as merely one human activity and interest among many, seems as remote from us as it was from Thackeray and the Victorians.

It may be we are living through a sexual revolution, amidst all the confusions attendant on revolution. It looks to me as though we are. If it is, whether we like the idea of it or not, we are all caught up in it, imaginative writers, just because they are imaginative writers, perhaps more than most people. Their degree of involvement, as writers, will, of course, vary enormously. I don't know how many English novelists would agree with Norman Mailer when he says of sex as a literary subject: 'I believe it is perhaps the last remaining frontier of the novel which has not been exhausted by the nineteenth and early twentieth century novelists.' When I read the remarkable fragment from his work in progress, *The Time of Her Time*, published in *Advertisements for Myself* (published, that is, in the American edition but not, repeat not, in the British, for self-evident reasons), I can see that it probably makes very good sense for Mr Mailer himself. But whether his generalisation is valid or not, every writer must decide for himself what are for him the limits of the permissible when dealing with sexual matters—or whether there should be limits at all.

The socially approved answer is easy: the permissible limits are passed when what results is pornographic or obscene. This doesn't help us much. Pornography and obscenity seem to me very different; but, beyond this, as soon as we try to define and discuss either of them, we find ourselves floundering in the morass of the subjective. The official objection to pornography is that it corrupts, presumably in that it leads those who read it to indulge in sexual practices they would not otherwise have thought of. There seems no very conclusive evidence that this is so, at least little evidence of greater weight than that represented by the juvenile delinquent who pleads in his defence that he 'saw it done on the telly'. So far as I know, none of the people who write about and against pornography admit to having been corrupted by it themselves; they merely believe that others are weaker and will be. In the absence of evidence, one can only be one's own guinea-pig.

Without pretending to a wide knowledge of pornography—pornography that is written at a level much above the barely literate is not in fact easy to come by—I think I can recognise it when I see it. It is fantasy writing, wish-fulfilment writing, differing from other forms of fantasy writing, such as romantic fiction, by being explicitly sexual. Unless the fantasies described chime with one's own line in fantasy—and I assume, perhaps rashly, that everybody has some kind of sexual fantasy—it will seem either comic or silly or repulsive, i.e., obscene. When the fantasies described chime with one's own the effect is masturbatory. Pornography is transcribed masturbation fantasy. It sets up, if you like, a vicious circle; but the more complex, the more elaborate, the more *recherché* the fantasy described, the more likely it is that its effects will stop at masturbation; if only because one of the sadder aspects of the more grotesquely perverse forms of sex is that to achieve them demands more time, more determination, and more money than are given to ordinary men and women.

If to corrupt means to lead to masturbation and if masturbation is a crime or a very evil thing, then those vigilant against pornography have a case. It would be a better case were it not obvious that throughout the ages masturbators have resorted to their practice without benefit of dirty books or dirty pictures. They aren't necessary at all. One knows very well that the mind intent on pornography will always find it, however innocent the material on which it is projected. One of the cherished possessions of the working class home of my childhood was a set of *Chambers's Encyclopaedia*. It contained colour-plates representing the peoples of the world which for two or three years were for me the furthest imaginable in lubricity, a bare-breasted Burmese lady smoking a cheroot, especially.

To conclude this excursion into the personal, I can only say that I have never found in any pornography I have read anything I had not been able to imagine for myself beforehand. Perhaps I have not read enough. But I should be surprised if this were not the common experience. Freud described the child as 'polymorphously perverse': we do not lose our polymorphous perversity all that easily or quickly.

Admittedly, there is a great deal of near- or sub-pornography around us today; there is also much material dressed up to look like pornography that is not pornographic at all; from the same motive, one supposes, as prompts the advertisers of beer and cigarettes to seek to identify their wares with images of a sexually excited or sexually satisfied couple. It is a solemn thought that, according to his publishers, the most widely read of living novelists is the American thriller-writer Mr Micky Spillane: he appears to have been translated into more languages than Shakespeare or indeed any other authors except Lenin, Stalin and Tolstoy. I confess to having read only one of Mr Spillane's novels. It ends with the hero shooting in the belly the villain, a beautiful female blonde psychiatrist (it seems somehow significant that she is a psychiatrist), with whom he has been to bed several times, as she strips in front of him in slow motion, the better, I suppose, to put him off his aim. I find Mr Spillane's work distasteful in the crudity of its sexual symbolism, to say nothing of its prose style, though not as distasteful as the fiction of our own Mr Ian Fleming. My reasons for disapproving more strongly of Mr Fleming are entirely priggish: he has had greater advantages of upbringing and education and should know better. But there it is. Mr Spillane, one understands, is the favourite light reading of ex-Vice President Nixon: President Kennedy relaxes from the cares of state with Mr Fleming; so who am I to complain? Mr Spillane's and Mr Fleming's books, with those of their fellow-travellers, are bought and read by millions throughout the world; and what are we to conclude from it? That Messrs Spillane, Fleming and the rest are debauching the millions by introducing them to the pleasures of sado-masochism of which they were formerly ignorant? It seems to me that all that is proved is that there are millions of men and women in the world whose sexual fantasies are sado-masochistic.

An addiction to pornography is no more commonly admitted than any other sexual vice. But we do know of one or two men who indulged in it. Of Richard Monckton-Milnes, first Baron Houghton, the *Dictionary of National Biography* says that he had 'many fine tastes, and some coarse ones'. He was the owner of one of the most famous nineteenth-century collections of pornography. Whether as a result he damaged his immortal soul one can only say, God knows. No one else does. It didn't prevent him from leading a public life of great value to the community as politician, man of affairs and as the generous friend and patron of poets. The nineteenth-century poet Coventry Patmore also had his collection of pornography, and this is the more piquant because he was the author of a very long poem, *The Angel in the House*, a celebration of the joys of domestic love. I thought once that this must argue hypocrisy in Patmore. It seems to me much more likely now that the interest in pornography was the shadow, to use Jung's word, of Patmore's insistence on the virtues of familial bliss which, I think it would be generally agreed, are rendered in over-sweet, nursery-milk-and-bread-and-butter terms; that the latter could not have been possible without the former. But, to complicate matters, after his conversion to Catholicism, Patmore became a mystical poet of real stature, with a much greater richness and depth than anything presaged in his domestic poetry.

I quote these instances not to do dirt on men of distinction but because we happen to know about them. It seems obvious that their addiction doesn't in any way affect the value of their life work. All one can say is that it was a matter for their own consciences, in other words, a purely private matter. Nor am I approving of pornography. Practically all that is displayed in bookstalls in this country and the United States is depressingly vulgar, unredeemed by wit or style. But that is an aesthetic, not a moral, judgment. I do not think we are in a position to make a moral judgment or, at any rate, a moral judgment of the kind that demands the invocation of the law. We do not know whether or in what sense or when pornography corrupts or tends to corrupt. All we can say with any confidence is that it has always existed and always will, so long as men and women have sexual fantasies they cannot realise, for whatever reasons, in actual life. It may, indeed, fulfil a social need, at the level, say, of the water closet and the public sewerage system. And we ought by now to know enough about human behaviour not to be too impressed by the zeal of those who would vindictively suppress what they consider pornography. We ought also, I think, to be very careful not to confuse questions of morals with questions of taste. As for the pornographers, I have never, so far as I know, met one. It must be a miserable trade, hawking the products of one's sexual obsessions in the streets; but I am not sure that I think it more miserable than some quite reputable commercial activities carried on by respectable citizens in order to turn an honest buck.

One thing I am quite sure of. Pornographic literature and literature as commonly understood have almost nothing in common. Writing conceived as art is in most ways the antithesis of pornography. It implies detachment, a rigorous exercise of the critical faculty, and the constant reference to observable reality. It is the opposite of unchecked fantasy and surrender to the obsessive. It has—or so serious writers themselves have always thought—something to do with truth, however private or fragmentary the truth may be.

Now the point of this consideration of pornography is that, when an author is charged under the Obscene Publications Act in England or under comparable statutes in other countries, it is really as a pornographer that he is tried. The law makes no distinction between pornography and obscenity; yet, while it is true, so much are we in the realms of the subjective here, that one man's obscenity may be another's pornography, the words are anything but synonymous. It seems to me that the distinction between them is valid and necessary. By derivation, pornography means, literally, brothel-writing, the description of the lives, manners and habits of prostitutes and their clients. Obscenity seems originally to have meant that which could not be represented upon the stage. It is related to ancient Greek theories of drama, according to which the plucking out of Gloucester's eyes in *King Lear* is obscene. By extension, the word covers a whole range of human functions which are neither good nor bad in themselves but natural, but which must be performed in privacy. They are obscene if they are not. The act of defecation is the obvious instance. The connotations of obscenity are far from being exclusively sexual. In origin, pornography is a concept in morals, obscenity a concept in aesthetics.

Observation seems to show that in literature the obscene almost invariably cancels out the pornographic. Swift is often undeniably obscene but when he is, the effect is the reverse of pornographic: it inhibits rather than enflames lust. To take a more recent instance, I assume that if James Joyce had stood trial at the Old Bailey the Gerty MacDowell episode in *Ulysses* is one of the passages he would have had to justify. It is a description of female exhibitionism and Bloom's masturbation in consequence. It could have been pornographic. It is anything but that, for the scene is rendered throughout in terms of irony, is disinfected as it were by comedy. It is satire on pornography. In my view, within the scope of Joyce's intention in the novel it is fully justified aesthetically. I do not see how it is possible to maintain that the passage tends to corrupt. But if it doesn't, what are the objections to it? There can be only one: that there are certain things in life, facts of existence known to every adult and to most children over the age of eleven or twelve, which must not be mentioned in imaginative writing. Simply, they must not be mentioned. And this, I suspect, is the attitude of the legal and the police minds, which, though one can think of many exceptions, are on the whole from their very nature repressive rather than permissive, reflecting current orthodoxies and even some no longer current in a form so distorted as often to amount to parody. When Mr Griffiths-Jones, leading for the prosecution in the *Chatterley* case, asked the jury in his opening address, 'Is this a book that you would even wish your wife or your servants to read?' more than one member of the jury must have wondered what century Mr Griffiths-Jones thought the trial was taking place in, or whether, indeed, he was wholly serious. Men and women have been writing poems, plays and works of fiction for the past forty centuries—and perpetrating pornography and obscenity too: it seems significant that it is only during the past century or so, since the ability to read became general, that books have been prosecuted for offending against morality; and one can scarcely help wondering whether at the root of these prosecutions there is not an unadmitted fear and distrust of the people construed as the masses, an obscure feeling that they need to be protected against themselves, that, in effect, as compared with those who rule them, their status is or ought to be that of wayward children. For it is to the putative effect of the book on a child that these cases always return. Mr Griffiths-Jones asked the jury another question: 'Would you approve of your young sons, young daughters—because girls can read as well as boys—reading this book?' We were back with Dickens:

> A certain institution in Mr Podsnap's mind which he called 'the young person' may be considered to have been embodied in Miss Podsnap, his daughter. It was an inconvenient and exacting institution, as requiring every-thing in the universe to be filed down and fitted to it. The question about everything was, would it bring a blush into the cheek of the young person? And the inconvenience of the young person was that, according to Mr Podsnap, she seemed always liable to burst into blushes when there was no need at all. There appeared to be no line of demarcation between the young person's excessive innocence, and another person's guiltiest knowledge. Take Mr Podsnap's word for it, and the soberest tints of drab, white, lilac, and grey, were all flaming red to this troublesome Bull of a young person.

It seems clear that while pornography, if my interpretation of what it is is correct, remains as it were constant, always the same, notions of what constitutes obscenity are always changing. What is socially per-missible changes from generation to generation. The Elizabethan dramatists, for example, enjoyed a freedom of expression beyond anything claimed by modern playwrights. I doubt if it would be possible for any dramatist of our time to allow his hero to talk to his heroine as Shakespeare makes Hamlet talk to Ophelia. Again, I fancy that the scatology of a poet like Pope strikes us as more obscene than it did his contemporaries. In an age when the staircases of great houses were used as public privies and chamber-pots were emptied from upper windows into the street below, men and women could hardly be squeamish about the simple bodily functions; but ours, with the universal provision of modern plumbing, is the age of the 'toilet' and the 'ladies' rest room'. On the other hand, much that we take as normal in our references to sex, spoken or written, would have seemed grossly obscene to the Victorians, though not to generations before them.

When prosecuting books of serious literary intention—*The Well of Loneliness, The Philanderer, The Image and the Search, Lady Chatterley's Lover*—the law may be seen as fighting a rearguard action against changing notions of the sexually obscene. The prosecution in the *Chatterley* case made much of Lawrence's use of the word 'fuck'. This is a word on which there has always been a most powerful tabu; it seems not to have been printed at all in English until very recently. But it is a word that all men know and that most have used. The notion that it is confined to the working class, especially to navvies and soldiers under the rank of officer, is, I believe, so much obscurantist nonsense; and now that the word is printed in books published by reputable publishers it is fascinating to see, from his autobiography *Growing*, Mr Leonard Woolf using it in a letter to Lytton Strachey in 1906. Mr Woolf is not a man whose interests suggest any close resemblance to navvies or private soldiers as traditionally imagined. When Mr Mailer's *The Naked and the Dead* was threatened with prosecution in 1949 it was largely because of the persistence with which he used, in the dialogue of his American soldiers, the adjective 'fugging', to denote the secondary usage of the forbidden word as a common swear-word made almost meaningless by constant repetition. The prosecution, it must be remembered, was threatened only in Britain; so far as I am aware, no such action or its equivalent was ever contemplated in the United States. But towards the end of the fifties, anyone like myself who habitually read American novels submitted to English publishers, usually in proof-form, could watch the forbidden word creeping into print and becoming, it seemed, almost obligatory in any novel that laid claims to realism. Usually, the offending word was cut out in the English edition. In 1959, however, it was allowed to remain in the English edition, put out by one of our oldest and most distinguished publishing houses, of J. G. Cozzens's best-selling novel *By Love Possessed*.

In these instances, the justification of the use of the word would be by the appeal to realism: this is the way men talk. In *Lady Chatterley's Lover*, Lawrence used it—much more frequently—for a quite different purpose. As Miss Helen Gardner said in evidence at the trial:

> I would like to begin by saying that I don't think any words are brutal and disgusting in themselves. They are brutal and disgusting if they are used in a brutal and disgusting sense or a brutal and disgusting context. I think that by the very fact that this word is used so frequently in the book, with every subsequent use the original shock is diminished, and I would say that by the end Lawrence has gone very far within the context of this book to redeem this word from low and vulgar associations, and to make one feel that it is the only word the character in the book could use. If one attempts to find any substitute I think it is impossible. By the time one reads the last page, Mellors' letter, this word has taken on great depth of meaning, has become related to natural processes, and is wholly justified in the context of this book. I don't mean I think Lawrence was able to redeem the word in usage. I am talking about its usage within the context of the book itself. . . . I think his intention was to make us feel that the sexual act was not shameful, and the word used in its original sense was not shameful either.

Lawrence's intention, then, was to restore the word in its original sense, and here his use of it is completely at odds with that of a naturalistic novelist like Mr Mailer. There is a problem here. Whether the word can be redeemed, in its public use, I would think doubtful. Its real value and importance lie in the fact that it is the only word we have for the performing of the act itself; everything else is periphrasis. And this suggests to me that in the interests of the language writers should be sparing of the use of the word in its secondary, swear-word sense. Most of the instances of its use I have come across in recent fiction seem to me trivial, unnecessary and artistically unjustifiable, inserted, one feels, 'for kicks' or to administer an adventitious shock to the reader. Writers have a duty here—to themselves and to writing; that is, if they regard themselves as more than purveyors of commodity goods. They mustn't let themselves be corrupted by what in effect are commercial practices. Some years ago, in my capacity as literary adviser to a publishing firm, I asked an American novelist, in many ways a good one and deservedly successful, why he found it necessary three or four times in every novel he wrote to bring in, often gratuitously, and describe a sexual encounter with a crudity and vulgarity that was plainly below his normal level of sensitivity. He replied that that was the way his American publishers, who knew what sold fiction, had taught him to write novels. Well, there is no law against the corruption of public taste, and I know no way by which the commercially minded can be stopped from cashing in on, exploiting and cheapening the freedom of expression honest men and writers have won for themselves at their own risk. And perhaps it doesn't much matter: books produced by their authors as consumer-goods sink without trace within a very few years.

My own view is that there is no aspect of human experience, however seemingly perverse, obscene or private, that is not fit material for art. But having said that, it seems to me that one must recognise that where rights are claimed obligations must be accepted. To take a subject which I think everyone would agree is an intensely private one, I can imagine a valuable novel being written about a woman's life which would deal in considerable degree with the fact and effects of menstruation. Of course it would need great literary skill and tact; it would also need genuine artistic integrity on the part of the writer. But these we have a right to demand from any writer who takes it upon himself to tackle a conventionally forbidden subject. He must accept full artistic responsibility for what he is attempting. It is his job to reconcile us to the forbidden, to humanise it and so bring it into the area of sympathetic understanding. This entails the absence of falsification by sensationalism, sentimentality or vulgarity. It entails aesthetic detachment, a pre-requisite of which is self-knowledge on the part of the author himself.

It is not a job for small writers; they had better remain in familiar territory. But it is what we have a right to insist upon. Indeed, we have to insist upon it, if we believe, as Wyndham Lewis said in *The Writer and the Absolute*, that

> There is in all those arts which parallel nature something like a law obliging the artist to a fanatical scrupulosity, as it were a physical incapacity to depart from nature's truth in exchange for any other. This is as inescapable as the requirements of geometry. The writer Flaubert as much as the painter Chardin provides an impressive illustration of this law. . . . The truth of the

great novelists is different from and more personal, certainly, than that of the contemporary 'scientific' historian. But in any case a meticulous fidelity to life is of its very essence. To ask it to falsify nature would be to destroy it.

If we don't believe that, I do not see what grounds we have for claiming for the writer unfettered freedom of expression.

CLAIRE RUSSELL

AND

W. M. S. RUSSELL

The Natural History
of Censorship

SOME thirty years ago, reviewing a new edition by Montague Summers of the works of Congreve, Lytton Strachey made a characteristic comment on the editor's treatment of a speech from *The Way of the World.* "'Tis true we found you and Mr Fainall in the blue garret,' says Mincing, the lady's maid, to Mrs Marwood; 'by the same token, you swore us to secrecy upon Messalina's Poems.' The learned editor had assumed this book to be 'a collection of obscene lyrics and songs clandestinely printed', and named in honour of the wayward Empress Messalina. 'Considerable research', he had added sadly, 'has failed to trace this book.'

> Alas, [wrote Strachey] Alas, for Mr Summers's 'considerable research'! . . . For the explanation is as simple as it is delightful: Mincing had got the title . . . just a little wrong; instead of 'Messalina's', she should have said 'Miscellaneous'. The difficulty of distinguishing between what is Miscellaneous and what is Messalina's is not confined to Mincing. The dividing line has never been absolutely drawn, and learned Magistrates are worried with the question to this hour.[1]

Drawing that line is the business of censorship, and so far, we must admit, it has been pretty wobbly. It is always jerking erratically about. The Obscene Publications Act of 1857 was given two totally different interpretations, by very distinguished lawyers, within eleven years.[2] It is all very easy on the face of it. We should like to encourage true communication, which helps to free people from their difficulties and make their behaviour more rational and unconstrained. We should like to discourage those processes of deception and seduction and propaganda which implant and evoke compulsive reactions. To regulate communication with these ends in view, all we have to do is to select the one thing and discard the other. All we have to do, in short, is to decide which is which.

Before we ask what on earth the learned Magistrates have to worry

[1] L. Strachey; Congreve, Collier, Macaulay and Mr Summers. The essay is reprinted in *Portraits in Miniature* (1931) and *Literary Essays* (1948). Chatto and Windus, London.

[2] P. Hartnoll (ed.) (1951) *The Oxford Companion to the Theatre.* University Press, Oxford: article on 'Dramatic Censorship' by M. E. Barber.

about, we had better take a look at some recent experiments carried out at the University of Michigan.[1] The experimenters reasoned that propaganda affects behaviour as poison affects the body. Now the most deadly poisons are substances very like those normally handled by the chemical reactions of the living body. Instead of being discarded from the system, such poisons are drawn into the machinery, and since they are, in fact, impostors, the machinery seizes up. On this analogy, it was predicted that propaganda would be most successful when it looks most like the victim's own impression of what is going on. Experiments were designed to test this hunch. For instance, subjects were asked to estimate the lengths of lines, while the experimenter, or a stooge in the know, offered alternative suggestions. It turns out that when these rival estimates are very different from the subject's own, he ignores them and confidently reiterates his own verdict. When they are very like his own, he *is* influenced, and no less confidently conforms to the suggestion from outside. When the difference is moderate, he tends to accept the propaganda and also to become uncertain and confused. After such experiments, we may well become a little uncertain and confused ourselves, and so will any censor who takes his work seriously.

Dividing Miscellaneous from Messalina's is evidently not as easy as it looked at first. Nothing daunted, every society has drawn its line. The trouble is that if we examine different societies, the line never seems to be in the same place. It would be well worth finding out which of these many censorships has done the best job, and why. After all, literature has had its ups and downs, and maybe different kinds of censorship have had something to do with this. But the first thing to do is to see how censorship works in practice, and whether it has ever been as rational and self-conscious as it usually claims to be. If not, we might realise that this is a problem for scientific research. So let us consider the natural history of censorship.

A society means a lot of individuals. Before we see how society goes about censorship, it may help to look at the problem in miniature, by seeing how the individual goes about it. For every man is his own censor, and has to regulate his intake of impressions and information. To begin with, he has to select from his sensations, and that means shutting some of them out. Even animals do this. For the most part, it is done for them by elaborate censoring machinery in their

[1] *Annual Reports of the Mental Health Research Institute*, University of Michigan, Ann Arbor: (1959) 3, pp. 12–13; (1960) 4, pp. 14–15.

brains; but sometimes they have to do it themselves. Take rats, for instance. Male rats, caged together, set up a simple society. The rank and status of individuals is sorted out in a series of wrestling matches, whose outcome establishes who can boss whom in the future. Each match ends in submission on the part of the loser. During the bout, the winning rat keeps his head down and fixes his eyes on his victim. The losing rat raises his head and gradually closes his eyes, thus shutting out the sight of his opponent. Eventually he sinks down and lies flat on his back, with eyes fully closed, straddled by the triumphant winner. Now if he had kept his eyes open and his head down, the sight of his victorious opponent would have triggered a compulsive reaction—headlong flight. Impelled as he is to play his part in the ranking match, and so to stay and submit, the loser must shut out the powerful temptation: so he raises his head and closes his eyes.[1]

This explanation of the losing rat's behaviour is, admittedly, still only a conjecture. But it looks more likely when we take into account an experiment performed by Emil Diebschlag on a pigeon.[2] The bird was trained to seek food at the centre of a spiral maze. Now birds learn such tasks in a positively bureaucratic way. They break the task down into a series of stages. The first job is to find the entrance of the maze. The sight of the entrance then triggers the second step—running right to the centre. Diebschlag's pigeon, on his way back to his home cage after a fruitful excursion into the maze, happened to pass near the entrance. In he went again! There was no food left there now, but the pigeon could not help himself. The sight of that entrance was an irresistible lure. He came out again, walked about, passed near the entrance again—and back in he went. After the sixth time round, Diebschlag had the definite impression that the bird tried hard to get back to his cage without going in sight of the entrance again, exactly like a reformed alcoholic passing a pub.

In the rat and the pigeon, shutting out one temptation is itself an automatic process, the result of some other impulse (such as wanting to go home) which is at least more appropriate at the time. Man, too, censors his sensations, and in similar ways. But here there are several possibilities. We may shut out sensations or take avoiding action in order to protect our rational function from the blind dictates of over-

---

[1] M. R. A. Chance (1962, in press) 'An Interpretation of Some Agonistic Postures: the Concept of "Cut-Off"'. *Symposia of the Zoological Society of London*, 8.

[2] Claire Russell and W. M. S. Russell *Human Behaviour: A New Approach*. Deutsch, London; Little, Brown, Boston (1961).

whelming stimulation. 'My blood begins my safer guides to rule', said Othello as he took in the deplorable scene of indiscipline at head-quarters in the middle of the night. As things turned out, he would have done very much better to go back to bed and sleep on it. There are homely enough examples of the rational shutting out of sensation. 'If I'd stayed there another moment, I'd have lost my temper and hit him'.... 'I shut my eyes and counted ten'.... It would be nice to be impervious to any provocations, but, at this stage of human evolu-tion, nobody is. It was with good reason that the resourceful Odysseus stopped his sailors' ears against the Sirens' song.

But this protective mechanism can run wild. If compulsions are rampant, more and more situations can pull the trigger. More and more casual combinations of words can arouse disturbing emotions. R. F. Benton asked human subjects to read pairs of words, which he flashed on a screen for very short periods. Each pair had to be flashed up a certain number of times in order to be read. Some words were unpleasant in themselves, others neutral. But a word neutral in itself might become disturbing if combined with another to produce some phrase of Freudian significance. If a neutral word was presented in one of these combinations, it took many more flashes to read it, than when it was presented in an innocuous phrase. Sometimes the subject's vision simply blurred. The upsetting phrase had somewhere been perceived, interpreted, linked with highly charged emotional con-ceptions—and then censored, all before the subject could read the phrase, and sometimes without his ever being able to read it.[1] A number of people, not unduly neurotic, were tested, and reacted in this way. But the loaded phrases were not the same for different people. Hence any piece of literature will have different irrational significance for different readers. As Lytton Strachey put it in the essay quoted earlier, 'the time, the place, the shifting significations of words, the myriad dispositions of the audience or the reader—all these things are variables which can never be reduced to a single formula'.

Nor is this all. There remains the process of projection—misinter-preting what one sees in the light or darkness of one's own compul-sions, ascribing one's own urges to others, seeing what is not there. This behaviour is so widespread that it forms the basis for many routine psychological tests, designed to show what different things different people see when none of the things are there. Like so much else, we owe this concept chiefly to Freud, though occasional instances

---

[1] Russell and Russell, *op. cit.*

were spotted before him. Ruskin, of all people, noted one in *Sesame and Lilies*: the aria 'La donna e mobile' in *Rigoletto*—'Wayward is womankind', as the old-world translation has it. Whether women are wayward or not, observed Ruskin, the source of the generalisation is suspect: the Duke, who sings the aria, is projecting his own colossal promiscuity. Projection is reduced to its absurd conclusion in the venerable joke about the patient asked to say the first word occurring to him in association to each of a series of words called out by his psychotherapist.

'Tree?'	'Sex'
'Table?'	'Sex'
'Chair?'	'Sex'
'House?'	'Sex' . . .

After about thirty words, the therapist regrettably loses his professional *sang-froid*, and remarks that the patient has an unusually one-track mind. 'But, doctor, it was you who brought up all those sexy words.'

Projection has obvious implications for censorship in individual and society. In Aldous Huxley's words, 'to the Puritan all things are impure'. Between them, projection and wholesale vulnerability to stimulation can cause the individual to censor out, not only sources of compulsive behaviour which do not mesh with his own brand, but also true information which might help to liberate him and encourage intelligent exploration. 'If it come to prohibiting,' wrote Milton in his *Areopagitica* pamphlet, 'there is not aught more likely to be prohibited than truth itself; whose first appearance to our eyes bleared and dimmed with prejudice and custom, is more unsightly and unplausible than many errors.' Or, in Oscar Wilde's less portentous phrase, we may end up by resisting anything except temptation.

For a long time past, it must occasionally have struck thoughtful people that the individual has regrettably little conscious control over the process that censors his impressions. But it was Freud who turned this uneasy feeling into a scientific demonstration, and systematically explored the automatic censor, notably in *The Psychopathology of Everyday Life* and in what he rightly considered his greatest book, *The Interpretation of Dreams*. He was concerned chiefly with the censorship of powerful emotional feelings and urges, of a compulsive nature, excluded from consciousness and creeping back to influence behaviour. The analogy was vividly present to his mind, and if we now use his work to throw light on censorship in society, we are only inverting his original train of thought. Finding that dreams expressed unconscious urges in distorted form, he asked himself: 'Where in social life can a similar mis-representation be found?' And he answered himself: in the work of a writer who is trying to smuggle banned ideas past a political censor. To make his point simply, he used the dream of an elderly and respectable widow, with grown-up sons serving at the Front in the first World War. She dreamed she went to the garrison hospital to offer her 'services'. As the long and detailed dream develops, it becomes clear what these services to soldiers are. Social censorship was such in Freud's day that he himself had to put them a little delicately, as 'love-services'. The dream contained a number of long conversations with various officers, to whom the lady explained her patriotic proposal. A little special censorship was expressed in the dream itself in her insistence that she was *not* prepared to serve 'a mere lad', showing plainly enough now (after Freud's work) that this dream is the old story of Jocasta's involvement with Oedipus. But whenever in these conversations a word or phrase occurred which would unmistakably betray the nature of the 'services', the dreamer ceased to hear herself or her interlocutors, and the talk became an unintelligible murmur. Freud compared this process of bowdlerisation to the work of a postal censor during the war, when he blocked out the words or phrases in a letter which he considered obnoxious.

From this starting-point Freud examined both the work of the automatic censor in the individual mind, and the manoeuvres of the censored or repressed compulsive urges in slipping through the censorship. He showed that the censor is vigilant and comprehensive in waking life: here the urges can only make a momentary appearance in the form of Freudian slips of the tongue or pen, which the individual can, as it were, disown. Such slips, he showed at length, were the *return of the repressed* urges, and this is certainly one of his most illuminating ideas. In the dream, however, he found perfect material for both aspects of his study. In sleep the censor relaxes, for the urges are now unlikely to find expression in extensive action: we can trace this principle even in animals.[1] But the repressed urges still do not have a completely free hand. And so a particularly interesting situation arises, in which they put their message across in a coded form, much as a skilful writer will convey his meaning in a code where nothing is ever sufficiently explicit to arouse the suspicions of the censor. Freud examined this coding process in detail, and broke it down into a number

---

[1] Russell and Russell, *op. cit.*

of particular coding techniques. First, there is condensation: the dream does not expound the whole message, but picks out a few key points. Then there is displacement: the images picked are not the obvious leading ideas of the message, and emphasis is ostensibly placed on the least important items. Then we have the elaborate devices of symbolism, where one thing stands for another. In the condensation process, the same original idea may be represented in several of the dream images, and conversely each image is chosen to suggest, by association, several of the original ideas: it is, as he put it, over-determined. The ingenuity of the coding process in some dreams was so outstanding that sometimes, like the ranks of Tuscany, Freud could scarce forbear to cheer.

In one way, this brilliant analysis was one-sided. Freud confined himself to studying the repression, and the return, of compulsive irrational urges. It is, however, clear from much evidence that the automatic censor in the individual represses other things as well—intelligent observations, imaginative trains of thought. The whole of Freud's analysis can be re-applied to this aspect of individual censorship, including the return of the repressed. The Freudian slip is by no means always a betrayal of irrationality. It may give vent to an accurate observation, even a psychoanalytic interpretation, of the behaviour of others. To illustrate this, we may mention a slip of tongue that produced the word 'bawdlerisation'. This is a perfect comment on the projections underlying the operations of Mr Bowdler on the plays of Shakespeare.

The return of repressed intelligence may take more complex forms than the slip of the tongue. We often make a true assessment of a situation, later repress it, and finally give expression to it after all. Shakespeare observed this sequence, and gave a fine example in *Hamlet*—only to be accused of inconsistency by those unacquainted with this mechanism. When Hamlet is about to leave for England with Rosencrantz and Guildenstern, he is in no doubt about their reliability and his own prospects. 'There's letters seal'd: and my two school-fellows,—Whom I will trust as I will adders fanged' . . . (Act III, Scene iv). In the same soliloquy, he even outlines a strategy—that of hoisting the engineer with his own petard. By the time he is on shipboard, he has repressed all this, and goes to his cabin to sleep. But the repressed intelligence is still at work. In his heart (as he tells Horatio in Act V), 'there was a kind of fighting, that would not let me sleep. . . . Our indiscretion sometimes serves us well, When our deep plots

F

do pall: and that should learn us There's a divinity that shapes our ends, rough-hew them how we will'. Restless with insomnia, he has a vague impulse to open the sealed letter from Claudius to the King of England. He does so, finds the order for his assassination, and proceeds to carry out the strategy he had formed in Denmark—without remembering anything about it. He substitutes for his own name those of Rosencrantz and Guildenstern. To him it seems like a new and strange inspiration: 'Ere I could make a prologue to my brains, They had begun the play,—I sat me down; Devised a new commission; wrote it fair' . . . and so on. The 'divinity that shapes our ends' turns out to be Hamlet's own intelligence. But the sequence of repression and return leads him to regard the final execution of the plan as an inspiration from outside. It is in this way that artists and scientists have conceived the notion of inspiring Muses.

Just like the repressed irrational urges, so repressed intelligence may find its outlet in the dream, a fact essential to the work of balanced dream-interpretation. Many examples are on hand of artists and scientists who have found their happiest 'inspirations' only in dreams. When these are analysed in detail, they are often found to use all Freud's coding devices for evading the censor. But sometimes they are much more explicit, and the censor relies on frustrating the dream by ensuring its repression when the dreamer awakens. The dreams we know about are the happy few that finally gave the censor the slip. The chemist Kekulé is well known for the discovery of the benzene ring, a particular arrangement of atoms which accounts for the properties of a large and important class of chemical substances. He was sitting at work on a textbook, but was making no progress: his thoughts wandered. He turned his chair to the fireplace and dozed off. The atoms flitted before his eyes. 'Long rows, variously, more closely, united; all in movement wriggling and turning like snakes. And see, what was that? One of the snakes seized its own tail and the image whirled scornfully before my eyes.' He abruptly awoke, and spent the rest of the night working out the consequences of the ring arrangement. 'Let us learn to dream, gentlemen', he ends the story.[1]

It is all very well to learn to dream, but the censor can make things pretty difficult. Otto Loewi, professor of pharmacology at the University of Graz, discovered the production, at the ends of certain nerve fibres, of chemical substances with drug-like effects, a finding of great importance for physiology and medicine. He woke up one night with

[1] Quoted in J. R. Baker (1942) *The Scientific Life*. Allen and Unwin, London.

a brilliant inspiration, and hastily jotted it down on a piece of paper. Next morning, alas, he could not decipher his own note. All day in his laboratory he racked his brains in vain. The following night the same thing occurred, and this time he carefully wrote down his idea before going to sleep again. Next day he went to his laboratory and performed one of the most beautiful and conclusive experiments in the history of science.[1] The poet Coleridge was less fortunate. In a farmhouse on Exmoor he fell asleep in his chair after reading a sentence from *Purchas's Pilgrimage* about the palace of Kubla Khan. He slept for three hours, and composed two or three hundred lines of poetry in his sleep. On waking, he eagerly began to write down the poem. 'At this moment he was unfortunately called out by a person on business from Porlock, and detained by him above an hour.' After the interruption, he could recall only a few scattered lines and images. He frequently planned to complete the poem, but he never succeeded; and thanks to the person from Porlock, we must be content with what we have of *Kubla Khan*.[2]

To be sure, there are ways of dealing with the person from Porlock. A person from Finland (a distinguished mathematician) came all the way to Paris specially to confer with Poincaré. The French genius was told of his arrival, but continued to pace up and down his study (as he did when working) for three hours, while the visitor waited humbly in the next room. 'At last the drapes parted and Poincaré's buffalo head was thrust for an instant into the room. "Vous me dérangez beaucoup" (You are disturbing me greatly), the head exploded, and disappeared. The caller departed without an interview.'[3]

Few of us are as ruthless as Poincaré. And anyway, this is no general solution of the problem. We must face the fact that, at present, the censor in the individual mind is beyond our control. That is why art is not yet a science, and science is still only an art. Perhaps it would not matter, if this censor did the job properly. But it is either undiscriminating, or even biased against intelligent creation. It is true that Freud has shown us how the censor is eluded in dreams, and how to assist this further by decoding them. It is true that prolonged psychoanalysis

[1] W. I. B. Beveridge (1957) *The Art of Scientific Investigation*. Third edition. Heinemann, London. A slightly different version is given by R. W. Gerard, in B. Ghiselin (ed.) (1955) *The Creative Process*. Mentor Books, New York. On the second night, according to Gerard, Loewi 'took no chances this time but went to the laboratory at once and started his experiment'.

[2] Quoted in Ghiselin, *op. cit.*

[3] E. T. Bell (1953) *Men of Mathematics. Vol. 2*. Penguin Books, Harmondsworth.

does seem to affect the censorship. But our ability to promote intelligent function in this way is still modest. It would help if we knew why some people do at least dream about benzene rings or Kubla Khan, while others do not. But at present we know next to nothing about the different kinds of censorship of intelligence that go on in different people. When we do, perhaps there will be some hope of releasing the enormous creative potential in human beings that is so largely wasted at present. In fine, censorship in the individual is automatic, it selects badly and falls lamentably short of the true goal, it varies considerably between different people, and we know very little about it.

Nearly all of what we have said so far can be transferred *en bloc* from the individual to the society. Repression of irrational compulsive urges occurs here too; so does the return of the repressed. Gibbon pinned down a beautiful example—the sudden outburst of image-worship in the Catholic Church, just after the final extirpation of paganism. As a pendant to this tremendous instance, we may add a microscopic one of our own. Any Londoner who wishes to see the return of the repressed, immortalised in stone, has only to visit Kew Gardens. 'Not far from the largest glass-house, there stands a crescent of stone figures. Each consists mainly of a head and bust rising from a simple stone column. The figures are evidently derived from those similarly truncated statues or busts of Hermes or the garden-god Priapus, which the ancients used to dot about their landscapes to encourage fertility among the plants therein. In order to convey this delicate hint, the statues (in ancient times) were always equipped with phalluses of generous and redoubtable proportions. The culture that constructed their modern equivalents at Kew had lost sight of the original function, and would certainly repress with Victorian fervour any such scandalous exhibitions (unless protected by the special licence accorded to the classics). There are no such phalluses at Kew. Hanging down each figure is a foliated leaf-like structure of considerable size, designed clearly to leave respectability doubly reassured, for what is not represented is hidden as well by this huge fig-leaf. But alas! you may repress fantasies with a pitch-fork—they will return as impudently as ever. The huge leaves turn up at the end and seem at this point to thicken and concentrate, so that there rises—from exactly the right place on each statue—a charmingly ritualised phallus.'[1]

Repression and return of the social expressions of intelligence are likewise to be observed in society. Indeed the Gibbon example is a

[1] Russell and Russell, *op. cit.*

mixed one, for the worship of images, pagan or otherwise, was accompanied by golden opportunities for exponents of the visual arts. Society too has its creative dreams; the dreams of art and science. It is true that science has evolved a method of linking its dreams together, to give a sort of cumulative effect. But the process is still distinctly haphazard. As in the individual, so in the society, we should like to bring these dreams to a more coherent life. Again the problem of censorship is central for the purpose. After what we have said about the individual, we cannot be very sanguine about censorship in the society. The growth of science has been one-sided; the course of art has been a series of interrupted spasms. There is little sign that censorship has been either rational or satisfactory upon the whole; and if censorship is automatic in the individual, it must be so *a fortiori* in the society. Again we see that societies have varied considerably, both in their censorships and in their creative output: but the relations between these two things are not at all simple or obvious. However, these relations may eventually provide us with an important clue. On, then, with our natural history of censorship.

The first thing the naturalist needs is a primitive system of classification. We can cross-classify censorships, splitting them in at least three ways. They may be formal or informal, prospective or retrospective, overt or covert. Prospective means selection in advance, retrospective means selection by suppression and/or punishment after the event. Formal censorship is exercised by definite legislation, informal censorship by other means. Overt censorship is aimed directly and specifically at communication. Covert formal censorship, in a sense always retrospective, is an interesting mechanism, with which we may begin. It is best explained by an example.

The U.S.A. is equipped with a large number of laws prohibiting various forms of sexual behaviour. Many of these laws have nothing directly to do with communication. The American Institute for Sex Research has estimated 'that 95% of the total male population could at some time be prosecuted as a sex-law violator of one sort or another'.[1] This means that these laws have relatively little effect in discouraging the practices at which they are ostensibly aimed. Their effect must be sought elsewhere. What they do achieve is to prevent people from comparing notes about their sexual behaviour, for anyone who talks about his sex life is likely to be confessing to a technical crime of one sort or another. Of course even this effect is by no means complete.

[1] V. Packard (1960) *The Status Seekers*. Longmans, London.

Moreover, since the covert prohibition is not backed by correspondingly thorough overt censorship, there was a way out of the dilemma, and it was found. By systematic assessment of information given in confidence, the Kinsey Reports let the cat out of the bag.

Prohibitive laws are always ostensibly designed to discourage and ideally eliminate some activity. It is interesting to notice that prohibition of this kind, combined with overt censorship, is in fact the means, often the only means, of perpetuating an activity. If left in the open, such doings might come to seem undesirable, and ways would be found of investigating and removing their real causes. This kind of prohibition is rather like rendering a building fire-proof by destroying the fire alarms. Moreover, it is a fundamental feature of human behaviour that the best way to put into any head an idea that was not there before is to mention it first as a prohibition. Fairy tales, wise in the ways of human nature, are always telling us about palaces with hundreds of rooms. As soon as we hear the fairy telling the prince that he must on no account open one of the several hundred doors, we know what will happen. Night and day, the thought of the forbidden room will obsess the hero, who would otherwise never have given it a thought. Before long, probably the day after the fairy's departure, he will go and open it. The mechanism is profound, predictable and pervasive. We experience it whenever we go to a dinner party where, for some reason or other, a particular topic must not be mentioned, for fear of embarrassing our hosts. No matter how the conversation drifts, it comes round inexorably, time and again, to the forbidden subject, which otherwise might be the last to arise. The mechanism has, of course, more important consequences. Prohibition of some activity, coupled with an implicit ban on talking about it, puts ideas into the heads of children, and imposes a subterranean urge to sample the forbidden fruit. It is thus a very important means of transmitting patterns of behaviour, otherwise liable to disappear, from generation to generation, by a process of behavioural inheritance.[1]

When people talk about censorship in society, they usually have in mind our next category—overt formal censorship, the official discouragement of certain kinds of communication. The selection may be exercised in advance by some licensing process, whereby, for instance, a book may only be published after submission to, and approval by, some official authority. Or it may be retrospective. Any book can be published, but if it is seditious, or heretical, or obscene,

---

[1] Russell and Russell, *op. cit.*, especially Chapter 4.

it is then suppressed, and sometimes the author and publisher punished. If such punishment is sufficiently ferocious, it may be a formidable deterrent, since the writing of a book is usually a less unreflecting activity than the commission of murder. Which method of censorship is adopted has a good deal to do with the medium of communication. Conversation can only be censored after the event, and the taboo words of simple illiterate societies are retrospectively enforced. In the ancient world, it was relatively easy to obtain and destroy most copies of a book, and the censorship of literature was largely retrospective. Printing means faster propagation: the bath may overflow before the censor can pull out the plug. The invention of printing was therefore followed by a wave of prospective censorship, dramatically described by Milton in his *Areopagitica*. The licensing of books was practised in late Tudor and in Stuart England. It has now disappeared, and the censorship of printed literature is entirely retrospective. Plays, on the other hand, if they are lucky, may be seen and heard by a substantial audience on the first night. The British theatre is still controlled by the Lord Chamberlain, as in Tudor times, and plays must meet his approval before they are performed in public.

But we should be greatly mistaken if we supposed that laws and official authorities are the only means of social pressure. A great variety of forces combine to make up an informal censorship, which may be very powerful. It may be prospective or retrospective, covert or overt. Some things just are not done; some things are just not talked about. And here it is much more difficult to find out just what is censored in a given society. Economic boycott is a useful index, but the means of enforcing informal censorship may vary from lynching to dirty looks. When Pericles (according to Thucydides) put forth his ideal of an uncensorious society, ostensibly as a portrait of Athens, he had all this clearly in mind. 'We have no black looks or angry words for our neighbour, if he enjoys himself in his own way, and we abstain from the little acts of churlishness which, though they leave no mark, yet cause annoyance to whoso notes them.'[1] It is an agreeable ideal, if hardly a faithful picture of the stormy city of Athens. It has, indeed, probably never been realised anywhere. Anyone who doubts the efficacy of informal censorship is welcome to defy it and see what happens. It is an ancient mechanism, evidently the oldest censorship of all. Something suspiciously like it turns up even in birds. The male

[1] Translation by Sir Alfred Zimmern (1961 Paperback), *The Greek Commonwealth·* Fifth edition, revised. University Press, Oxford.

spice finch is given to uttering a complicated song, which has been called a Jingle, and which includes 'a miscellany of high-pitched, flute-like, whistles, mingled with harsh, low-pitched, loud Slurs . . . and a peculiar bill-rattling produced by very rapid opening and closing of the bill'. When one of the males is sounding off in this way, another bird may fly up and join him. The new arrival (who may be called the 'Reactor') *peers* closely into the singer's face. The singer 'tries to move his head away, or, as this is seldom sufficient to deter the Reactor, edges away along the branch, continuing to Jingle as he goes. But the peering bird usually follows, and the two may sidle a considerable distance side by side, the Reactor still peering at the performer and occasionally pecking him on the top of the head, the neck, or, rarely, in the region of the tail base or vent. . . . Such constant interruptions by the Reactor may force the performer to stop Jingling, or even to fly away. Should the performer start again after a brief delay, the Reactor is usually on to him at once. . . . There are sometimes two simultaneous Reactors to one performer. The course of events is then much as usual, although the Reactors tend to get in one another's way.'[1] This merciless persecution has been called 'peering', and it seems no wonder the performer is put off. The censorious bird is unlikely to be prompted by aesthetic feelings about high-pitched whistles, low-pitched Slurs and peculiar bill-rattling. The reason for peering appears from another reaction which may also occur: instead of peering, the second bird may join in the song. It appears that this Jingle (like some others we know about) is infectious, and induces compulsive behaviour. The censor is protecting himself against this by a more active version of the shutting-out behaviour we considered earlier. Informal censorship in man may often be understood in this way, as we have also seen, but is unfortunately not confined to resisting Jingles.

In fact, as long as social censorship of all these kinds is automatic, it tends indiscrimately to resist any source of disturbance to the society's own pattern of automatic behaviour. As in the individual, so in the society, the disturbance may come from either rational or rival irrational influences. Sometimes the resistance becomes extreme and all-pervasive; then literature declines. Sometimes the social censorship

[1] M. Moynihan and F. Hall (1954) 'Hostile, Sexual and other Social Behaviour Patterns of the Spice Finch (*Lonchura punctulata*) in captivity'. *Behaviour*, 7, pp. 33–76. There are photographs of peering spice finches in D. Morris (1958) 'The Comparative Ethology of Grassfinches (Erythrurae) and Mannikins (Amadinae)'. *Proceedings of the Zoological Society of London*, 131, pp. 389–439.

may let through some material which seems innocuous, either because it is unlikely to take effect, or because change is already on the way, and cannot be averted any longer. We then have a period of relatively rich literary output. But the nature of this output varies in different periods, as the focus of censorship shifts to different sources of disturbance.

Consider for a moment two periods of literary, and especially dramatic, flowering: fifth-century Athens and Elizabethan (and early Jacobean) England. In the literature and drama of these times, we can discern a certain freedom in the treatment of sexual behaviour. We may suppose that neither society felt threatened by this: as a component of the social structure, sexual behaviour seemed to be under control. But the full weight of censorship, formal and informal, was brought to bear upon criticism, rational or irrational, of the political activity and religious beliefs of the state. Could an Elizabethan have dipped into Victorian literature, he might have smiled at its sexual prudery; he would have started at its frankness on matters of politics and religion. In Elizabethan England, formal censorship, prospective and retrospective, was sharp enough on these points. It was not enough that new plays were censored in advance: unfortunately-timed production of an old one could get a company into serious trouble. The playwrights used contemporary English settings only in social comedies far removed from high matters of state policy. But the authorities were on the watch for symbols and allusions too. During the revolt of the Earl of Essex, they pounced on a revival of *Richard II*, in which a king of England is deposed. The greatest ingenuity was required to comment on the political scene without appearing to do so.

In the democracy of Athens, informal censorship prevailed. But retrospective formal methods were available at need. A distinction seems to have been drawn, in the fifth century, between the two principal kinds of play. By long-standing ritual tradition, it was generally agreed that jokes about the gods meant no harm, and were not to be taken seriously. The principle seems to have been extended to jokes about the democracy and its terrestrial leaders. The comedy of this period was particularly free, though even a comedian ran the risk of prosecution by some indignant demagogue. In tragedy, which was taken seriously, one had to be more careful. Phrynichus wrote and produced a tragedy on an incident of near-contemporary history. His subject, the capture of Miletus by the Persians, happened to be a sore one at Athens. The citizens fined him, and decreed that no-one should ever revive the play. After that, the tragedians tended to use contemporary settings only in dealing with agreeable subjects (like Persian defeats), and otherwise to concentrate on setting stories of remote and legendary antiquity. Piety was another knotty point, and criticism of the gods in tragedy was as suspect as criticism of the democracy itself. The playwrights still tried to comment on contemporary beliefs and practices, but did so by allusion and parallel. Euripides did this too clumsily for an Athenian audience, as quick to spot symbols as the Elizabethans. His ancient wars looked too like modern ones. He won few dramatic awards, and became increasingly unpopular. In the end he went abroad, perhaps to escape 'black looks', 'angry words' and 'little acts of churlishness'.

Sophocles, less clumsy, enjoyed unrivalled popularity and success. Nevertheless, his plays express profound observation of the contemporary scene. Shakespeare was another who kept out of trouble, though the difficulty became too much even for him at last, and, unlike the Athenian, he finally retired from the stage. When we see how these two great writers eluded and baffled the social censorship to which they were exposed, we are reminded of those particularly clever dreams which aroused the admiration of Freud. As in the dreams, so in the plays, we can watch the coding process at work. The same principles of condensation, displacement and symbolism appear in both.[1] One example will suffice to illustrate the point.

There are several reasons for assigning to the year 1601 the composition of *Hamlet*. At this time a chief topic of interest for thoughtful Englishmen was the history and personality of James VI of Scotland. If civil war was to be averted, it was important for him to succeed the ageing Elizabeth I on the English throne. It is also known that a troupe of English actors, closely associated with Shakespeare, visited James in Scotland that year; and there are even less certain grounds for conjecture that Shakespeare himself was among them.[2] Now the circumstances surrounding the King's parents were, to say the least, dramatic. His father, Lord Darnley, had been murdered. His mother, Mary, Queen of Scots, had subsequently married the man accused by popular rumour of the murder, and was widely believed to have been herself an accessory before the fact. Unfortunately rumour also had it

---

[1] Russell and Russell, *op. cit.*, especially Chapters 8 (Sophocles) and 9 (Shakespeare).

[2] C. Longworth de Chambrun (1957) *Shakespeare: a Portrait Restored.* Hollis and Carter, London. This well-documented fact was unknown to us when we made this analysis of the play (Russell and Russell, *op. cit.*).

that James was the illegitimate son of another lover of this undiscriminating queen. His claim to both English and Scottish thrones was
undermined by such talk. Although he had made only half-hearted
attempts to save her life when she died on an English scaffold, he was
extremely jealous of her reputation. In 1596, he obtained an Act
making it treasonable to slander the King's parents or progenitors, and
at least two people were hanged at Edinburgh under the Act. In the
same year, he objected to the sorceress Duessa in Spenser's *Faerie
Queene*, as a portrait of Mary, and asked Elizabeth (in vain) to punish
the poet. He was thus at once a dangerous and an irresistible subject
for a play.

It seems at first sight incredible daring on Shakespeare's part to
present a hero with a murdered father and a mother married to the
murderer. As if this were not enough, *Hamlet* is set in Elsinore, where
some years previously James had been entertained to a feast in celebration of his marriage to a Scandinavian princess. The play actually
begins with just such a celebration. Yet, as we know, Shakespeare got
away with it. He did so by condensation. Hamlet is linked to James
by his situation. But his personality is different in every way, and links
him to two other people. In his alternate outbursts and hesitations, he
at once recalls Elizabeth I, with whom he shares such traits as jotting
down notes and thrusting his sword through the arras. In his passion
for the theatre, he plainly reflects the author himself. Thus one character represents three different people. Conversely, James is represented by
four characters in the play. He shares with Hamlet his family situation,
with Fortinbras his destined role as the uniter of two kingdoms, with
Claudius his views on the divine right of kings (and other more disagreeable qualities), and with Polonius his taste in theatrical performance—he liked spectacle and disliked long plays, in itself a sign of
increasing censorship, which in his English reign was finally to prove
too much for Shakespeare. By covering his tracks in this way, Shakespeare was free to express a great deal of what he saw and felt about
the impending reign.

It is not easy now to disentangle, in the coding processes of Sophocles
and Shakespeare, conscious from unconscious artifice. We do not know
how far their individual censorships conformed to the social one.
Berthold Brecht appears to have admired Stalin: yet in one of his plays
he introduces a tyrannical governor of Tiflis (Stalin's home-town)
with a name recalling the dictator's, and displays that governor's
severed head upon the stage. It is not always clear, when repressed

intelligence returns, whether it is slipping past the individual or the social censor. There is certainly a very close relation between the two, as is obvious from the existence of informal censorship, exercised through the reactions of individuals. The same sexual restrictions, which controlled the dreams of Freud's patients, controlled the literature of the later nineteenth and early twentieth centuries.

It is also clear how perfect at all points is the parallel between the return of repressed irrational and rational material. Whether the dreamer or the poet is seeking to express compulsive urges or imaginative observation and feeling, he uses the same devices to elude his own and society's censor. We have seen how the artist or scientist is led to ascribe his own discoveries to outside inspiration. Social censorship directed at intelligence will lend point to the alibi. To both internal and external censor, the artist may put forward a plea in mitigation: 'I had nothing to do with it, I was the innocent instrument of a power outside myself.' Just so may the delinquent plead, ascribing his irrational and destructive acts to compulsion by forces outside his personality: 'I couldn't help myself, something came over me.' Again the plea may be made before either tribunal, or both. The social censorship, thwarting both delinquent and creative enterprise, forces them to behave in exactly the same way. It is a vicious circle. For the two things, which rational regulation would distinguish, come to look more and more alike in their individual and social expressions.

In fine, all social censorships have failed to draw the line between the creative and the compulsive. Instead, each has drawn its line between its own pattern of belief and behaviour, and any others, intelligent or otherwise. Each society, or each phase of a changing society, has its own pattern; that is why, as we remarked at the outset, the lines are never in the same place. That is why they are always shifting.

We are liable to mistake these shifts for absolute progress. We tend to feel that we must be, socially and individually, altogether less irrationally restricted than, say, our Victorian forebears. The notion is misleading, and makes things very easy for our present irrational censorships. The record of the past shows that, while censorship remains automatic, it never truly gives ground: it only shifts it. The Victorian freethinker might pique himself on his sceptical writings, unthinkable in Elizabethan days, as he sampled Mr Bowdler's new version of the plays of Shakespeare. The modern American psychiatrist can afford an indulgent smile at Victorian sexual pruderies. But he sometimes tends 'to react with embarrassment when the question of social class is raised':[1] a question discussed with considerable freedom by Victorian novelists and thinkers.

As social censorship comes to change in this way, individual censorship changes too. But some individuals move ahead of their society, while others lag behind. The former are not, as we have just seen, truly more advanced: but they are no longer subject to the original restrictions. The dreams of the individual are planned with his own censor in view. Another person, whose internal censor has already moved on, may find them transparent. Thus could Freud decode the dreams of his Viennese patients, as an early representative of that new form of society into which the old one was already changing. In doing this, he gave us basic principles of coding and decoding. But the nature of the code he cracked, reflecting the particular pattern of the censorship, is another matter. Some modern individuals still live in the Victorian age, and have Victorian dreams, for which Freud has provided the decoding key. But social censorship has moved on, and with it those of many individuals. It is not much help to know what innocent symbols stand for sexual intercourse, when the modern patient dreams of sexual intercourse itself.

Before we ever get a rational regulation of literature, selecting the creative from the compulsive, we shall have to unmask the automatic censorships that continue to make quite different selections. When Freud unmasked the Victorian variety, it was already in process of changing its shape. Obviously it is of first importance to establish what is actually censored in *our* societies. But this, from the nature of the case, it is particularly difficult to discover. Censorship is like the god Proteus, guardian of the answer to certain questions, who eluded the grip of the questioner by ceaseless metamorphoses. We have seen that censorship never gives ground, but only shifts it. Victorian prudery may be a thing of the past, but what has taken its place? Nor is even the ground apparently yielded necessarily finally won. We cannot assume complete modern enlightenment on even the matter of sexual behaviour. There are ways and ways of repressing the same thing. No subject will be altogether immune from automatic censorship, until all subjects are. The censor guards the vast and intricate mechanism of society, in which all the parts are interconnected in a puzzling network. The censor can afford to let us look at one part—it will distract us, while he quickly covers up another. It will not profit

[1] A. B. Hollingshead, quoted in Packard, *op. cit.*

us much, for we shall not understand the first part without seeing its connection with the second. As long as any part of the machine is shielded, we shall never fully grasp the functions of the other components. Nor is even this all. History records many fluctuations in the censorship of particular subjects. Victorian prudery might quite conceivably return, unless we can solve the problem whole. In shifting his ground, the censor can turn on his tracks.

The natural history of censorship affords one clue at least to this labyrinthine problem. We should not be exclusively obsessed with formal legislation. Ambiguous as it often is, it is in the open: informal censorship, subtle and pervasive, is hiding all around us, permeating even the figures of everyday speech. In the exploration of informal censorship lie the greatest perplexities and the greatest potential rewards. Our questions must be addressed, not only to the learned Magistrates, but also to that busy if enigmatic individual, the Man in the Street. Where, by the way, is his colleague, the Woman in the Street? She never seems to be about. She never has been, either: so it can't be the fault of the Wolfenden Report.

JOHN CHANDOS

Unicorns at Play

'**O**BSCENE writing' is primarily divisible into two classes, which for the purpose of this examination I will call 'offensive' and 'alluring'.

The effect of the former upon those most vulnerable to it is to cause a disagreeable, even distressing shock to the feelings by the presentation of indecent and forbidden words or images. The effect, or conjectured effect, of the latter class upon hypothetically 'susceptible' minds is, as its name implies, to tempt or draw such minds to the enjoyment of thoughts (and perhaps to consequent actions) of a libidinous nature, or by persuasive arguments to win over such minds to beliefs and conduct which the arbiters of morals, whoever they may be, consider undesirable.

On occasions the two classes overlap, and may be found sometimes united in a single work. De Sade's *Justine* is an example of such 'comprehensive obscenity'. It contains language and terms which constitute strong 'offensive' obscenity; at the same time it could allure by the detailed descriptions of certain sexual transactions and it might 'corrupt' by the reasoned arguments it offers in support of these practices.

Obscenity, whether naked or veiled, is an elemental force in the art of all psychologically healthy societies. It is in the nature of art to transmute vitality and conflict into revelation, and it is the commitment in depth of art, not any limitation of subject matter, which distinguishes literature from pornography.

The obscene element in *Lolita*, for example, is indispensable to the story; it is also ideal material for pornography. But in *Lolita*, what happens is that the 'obscenity', instead of being isolated on a treadmill of erotic intent, is made free to retrace the course of its fantasy until it is reabsorbed by the tragi-comic humanity of the author's understanding.

This process of transmutation is familiar to anyone with the least responsiveness to literature, and would not merit a sentence of space here but for the fact that there have been and are highly vocal readers who are exclusively and obsessively conscious, either censoriously, or pruriently, or both, of obscenity.

The Duke de la Meilleraye, in inheriting a share of Mazarin's art treasures through his wife, Hortense Mancini, mutilated with an axe all the male statues. His prudish aggression was eccentric in his time; by the nineteenth century it would have been orthodox and commonplace.

Pornography and erotica, as opposed to literature with bawdy or erotic content, did not gain currency until the nineteenth century. But strong and frank language clashed in free and open contest. In 1764 Charles Churchill, taking aim at homosexuality, wrote

> Go where you will, at every time and place
> Sodom confronts and Stares us in the face
> They ply in public at our very doors
> And take the bread from much more honest whores.
> Those who are mean high paramours secure
> And the high guilty screen the guilty poor.
>
> Women are kept for nothing but the breed,
> For pleasure we must have a Ganymede,
> A fine fresh Hylas, a delicious boy
> To serve our purposes of beastly Joy.

Before Victoria had ascended the throne, Churchill's and other critical and satirical works of the eighteenth century, written with the intention of reforming manners and correcting morals, had themselves become 'obscene', unendurable to the Victorian conscience. In the interval homosexuality had not ceased but, on the evidence, increased; it had become socially impermissible, however, to refer to its existence. Allusion to relations between the sexes was almost as equally inhibited.

> If an Englishman of today were to write like Catullus of Herrick, or tell such tales as La Berceau of La Fontaine, or the 'Carpenter's Wife' of Chaucer, we should hound him from our libraries, and justly: because no Englishman in the presence of our civilization with the advantages of our decisive finalities as to the decencies of language could say to his conscience, 'I have a right to say these things.'[1]

Thus when, two years after that pronouncement of Buchanan's was written, a group of Oxford classical scholars translated and had privately printed the verses of Martial normally omitted from the Bohun and other contemporary English translations, they felt obliged

[1] Robert Buchanan. *The Fortnightly.* 15th Sept. 1866, Vol. VI, p. 297.

to keep their identity secret. Their anonymous voice in the introduction to this work speaks for the submerged and suppressed in Victorian life:

> There is a superficial morality among the English of the present day, which unhappily bears all before it, and those who dare to write in the teeth of this bring upon themselves most unmerited obloquy; the consequence of this is shown in all our translations of the classics. . . .

The insatiable sex-consciousness caused by these inhibitions drove out the forbidden image from one scene after another, but always the apparition returned elsewhere. Expelled from literature, it materialised in the food on the table and it became indelicate to ask for a 'breast' of chicken or 'leg' of lamb.

It was in such soil and climate as this, enjoying the advantages of these 'decisive finalities' of moral propriety, that pornography took root in England and flourished as never before. Before the reign of Victoria, much of what we would call obscenity was non-erotic, and appeared openly as part of the armoury of invective and abuse employed in the course of political and private feuds, and what was erotic was dressed in the language of literature.

The first example of predominant obscenity as, one might say, 'constructive pornography' was the Earl of Rochester's play *Sodom*. The theme of the play was the tyranny of a paederastic monarch, King Bolloxinian who forbids all normal sexual transactions and enforces homosexuality by law. Other characters include General Buggeranthos, Pimps of Honour, Vertuoso, Merkin and Dildoe maker to the Royal Family, and Flux, a physician.

The play opens in the royal palace with the news of the arrival of gifts from a neighbouring sovereign.

> *Courtier:* My liege, a stranger at yon royal gate
> Does from Gomorrah with a message wait
> And forty stripling for a present bring.
> *King:* Oh it's a present from our brother king.
> Conduct them in, 'twas very kindly done.

The whole thing becomes as gross as Rochester's infantile sexual fantasy can make it, but the style is still the style of literature and there is some merit in the verse as a parody of Dryden.

In the end the King refuses to restore the natural moral order whereupon thunder is heard and fiery demons rise and sing menacingly, then vanish in smoke to be succeeded by the ghost of the Queen who brings her surviving spouse his final warning.

> *Queen:* Tyrant thy day of doom is now come
> My wretched fears
> Thy want of penitence and tears
> I know Hell's Plagues partake
> For thy Damned sake.
> We'll shortly meet again
> With Howlings plagues and pain.

At these words 'dreadful shrieks and groans are heard and horrid apparitions are seen', but the King remains unrepentant and proclaims his intention of retiring into a last-stand bunker.

> Let Heaven descend and set the world on fire,
> We to some darker cavern will retire.

At the time *Sodom* was an isolated freak and its interest lies in its being the first of its kind and in the significance of its subject matter. Homosexual practices must have been familiar among the upper classes and at Court for *Sodom* to have been a realisable concept, and there is no lack of testimony, quiet and loud, to confirm that this was so. Pepys, prudent man, hinted it. 'He tells me that the kings and court were never in the world so bad as they are now, for gaming, swearing, women and drinking and the most abominable vices that ever were in the world.' Later voices were louder and unequivocal. 'Vile catamites make their preposterous addresses even in the very streets.'[1] But few powerful men suffered; they were protected or protected themselves. When 'Beau' Wilson, a strikingly handsome young man at the court of Charles II was killed in a duel with John Law, and certain compromising evidence circulated, an anonymous publication appeared, *Love Letters between a Certain late Nobleman and the famous Mr Wilson* a safe distance of time afterwards, but that was all. In the following century, when a satire against David Garrick, *The Lamentation of Roscius for his Nycky*, appeared, David Garrick bought up five editions as fast as they appeared, while his 'Nycky' (Isaac Bickerstaff) cleared off to St Malo for a change of air.

The lower orders, who must have provided much of the manpower in these circles, were more accessible to vengeance, and periodical swoops took place, organised by informers. Such accomplices, then as now, enjoyed ambivalent rewards, being often accomplices and

[1] Saton's *Harvest Home*, 1749.

blackmailers of those on whom they finally informed. Their evidence was glib with professional unction. A woman employed in the Golden Ball in Bonds Stables near Fetter Lane, having kept watch through a crack in the wall upon a scene in a private room, raised the alarm with the cry, 'I can look no longer, I am ready to swoon.' In 1725 there was a raid upon a house kept by a woman known as Mother Clap in Field Lane off Holborn, 'next the Bunch of Grapes on one side and joined to an arch on the other side', which was the resort of what were then called 'Molly-culls' or 'Mollies'. At her trial in July 1726 an informer deposed that forty to fifty men in the room would sometimes 'sit on each other's laps' and behave 'in a lewd manner'. Then they would get up, dance and make curtsies and mimick the voices of women. 'O, Fie, sir,'—'Pray, sir,'—'Dear sir,' 'Lord how can you use me so?' 'I swear I'll cry out,'—'You're a wicked devil,'—'And you're a bold face,'—'Eh, ye little toad, come buss!' Then they'd hug and play and toy, and go out by couples into the room on the same floor, to be married, as they called it. . . .'

A much later raid obtained special notoriety because of the offer by the prisoner Cook in the course of his defence to turn King's evidence and betray his high-placed clients—an offer which was refused. Most of those arrested conducted the offending side of their lives under assumed—female—names. 'Kitty Cambric' was a coal merchant, 'Miss Selina' a runner at a police office, 'Black-eyed Leonora' a drummer, 'Pretty Harriet' a butcher, 'Lady Godiva' a waiter, 'the Duchess of Gloucester' a gentleman's servant, 'the Duchess of Devonshire' a blacksmith, 'Miss Sweetlips' a country grocer, 'Fanny Murrey' an athletic bargeman, 'Lucy Cooper' a herculean coalheaver, 'Kitty Fisher' a deaf tyre-smith.

It is necessary to be aware of this aspect of the sexual underworld of England before the reign of Victoria to understand the variety of shapes into which Victorian pornography grew. But to return to the mainstream of the subject we must go back to the middle of the eighteenth century and the appearance of the first—and many people think the best—English erotic work. It was written in a debtors' prison by John Cleland for £20, and yielded the publishers a profit of £10,000: sums which should be multiplied by ten to estimate their contemporary value.

The Memoirs of a Lady of Quality, or *The Memoirs of Fanny Hill*, as it is even better known, recounts the adventures of a pretty and high-spirited Lancashire girl who comes to seek her fortune in London after the death of her parents. There is nothing in English to prepare us for it. Curle and other disreputable publishers had produced lewd, outrageous books, but their main offence, it should be remembered, was political; their productions were not erotic, *alluring*. *Fanny Hill*, as we may conveniently call it, stands alone in its time in English; but long after it became the model for all kinds of imitations in England and America, diluted like spirits to varying degrees of libidinous strength from the 'over-proof' *Memoirs of a Voluptuary* to the safely watered *Forever Amber*.

Despite the circumstance in which it was written there is no sign in the book of haste or carelessness. It moves with a racy yet elegant confidence, and a polished felicity of phrase which occasionally, as if to show what the author could do if he would, makes a sally across the border and into the climate of literature. Such excursions, however, are tantalisingly brief; *Fanny Hill* is predominantly an erotic work from start to finish. The narrative sketches introducing each new character or situation are consummately skilful but they are never developed. We are stimulatingly told what people are like, but never shown them being or becoming anything for longer than a fleeting moment other than protagonists in a succession of venereal contests.

A hint of what Fanny Hill might have been is given in the description of Esther, the actress who travelled with Fanny on the coach to London and told her 'after her manner and style'—evidently actresses were affected in speech even then—

> as how several maids out of the country had made themselves and all their kin for ever: that by preserving their *vartue* they had taken so with their masters that they had married them and kept them coaches, and lived vastly grand and happy; and some mayhap came to be Dutchesses; luck was all, and why not I as well as an other?

Arrived in the frightening, tumultuous metropolis, Fanny goes in search of work to an 'intelligence office' where she innocently allows herself to be picked up by an old bawd, and accepts an offer of employment without appreciating the nature of the establishment in which she is to serve.

In the brothel Fanny learns much by means of stealthy observation (all described in detail) but retains her virginity—lesson: do not be in a hurry to commit the persons of your main protagonists—and then one day she meets the man of her life, an Adonis whom she first sees alone and asleep on a chair in a room of the house after a night of carousel with boon companions. It is 'love at first sight' and later with his assistance she escapes from the house.

> And now, got safe into the street I saw my new guardian angel waiting at a coach door, ready open . . .
> I was in the coach in a trice, he by the side of me, with his arms clasped round me, and giving me the kiss of welcome. The coachman had his orders and drove to them.
> In an instant, for time was annihilated with me, we were landed at a public house in Chelsea, hospitably commodious for the reception of duet parties of pleasure, where a breakfast of chocolate was prepared for us.
> An old jolly stager, who kept it, and understood life perfectly well, breakfasted with us and, leering archly at me, gave us both joy and said 'We were well paired, i' faith! that a great many gentlemen and ladies used his house, but he had never seen a handsomer couple . . . he was sure I was a fresh piece . . . I looked so country, so innocent! Well, my spouse was a lucky man! . . .' all which common landlord's cant not only pleased and soothed me to divert my confusion at being with my new sovereign whom, now the minute approached I began to fear to be alone with: a timidity which true love had a greater share in than even maiden bashfulness.

It will be seen that Cleland invokes the name and appearance of sentimental love, which common pornographers seldom do, but this is just clever decor and dressing for the main action. Cleland knew perfectly well that Eros in love changes his nature, and that Fanny truly depicted in love, would not, could not, have registered her experiences in the terms that he needs must make her do. She must therefore say one thing and act another when the critical time approaches

> After breakfast *Charles* (the dear familiar name I must take the liberty henceforward to distinguish my Adonis by), with a smile full of meaning, took me gently by the hand and said, 'Come my dear, I will show you a room that commands a fine prospect over some gardens . . .'

After the conventionally painful though gladly made surrender of her virginity, Fanny settles down with Charles in great contentment. But this situation does not serve the purpose of the story so Charles has to be got rid of, temporarily at least, and his father obliges by having him kidnapped and shipped off to the West Indies, to further, he hopes, his own chances of a legacy, leaving Fanny alone and penniless. By the contrivance of a mercenary landlady threatening her with a debtors prison, Fanny is forced into the arms of a rich protector who has, for some time passed, admired her from a distance. He is generous, kind and aristocratic, and after her gradual recovery from the horror of physical intimacy with anyone other than her adored Charles, she learns to tolerate her life well enough. Then one day she observes her lover amusing himself with her own maid and in revenge she entertains herself by seducing his manservant, an adolescent priapic Hercules. Indulging once too often a taste for the person of this awakening giant, Fanny is surprised by her protector *in flagrante delicto* and dismissed, though not without generous provision being made for her immediate needs. Now she finds herself alone again but no longer helpless; she has some money and more experience, and thus she is launched upon the career of sensuality which it is the purpose of this book to chronicle.

The Memoirs of Fanny Hill may be taken as an epitome of erotic books. It is better written than most and employs with craft all the basic moves and devices for rousing the feelings, holding the attention and provoking the curiosity of the reader, which have been subsequently imitated by other hands. It also displays, the clearer for its merits, the central defect of all writing which is predominantly erotic or pornographic in intent, a total absence of organic vitality. A scene is set, a performance is projected, but at the end our hearts are unmoved; we know we have not been in touch with a living process. No prospect remains but an empty stage awaiting another ephemeral performance. Cleland rings the changes in decor and physical appearance; Boccaccio-like he moves the point of view by introducing new characters to tell their several stories; he punctuates the most animated struggles with breathing-spaces of ease and meditation; he calls up diversions of paederasty and curiosities of perversion, and drives the main action to its climax in an ambitious set-piece, an orgiastic party at which selected partners vie in comradely rivalry to produce the most piquante and original acts.

But despite the ingenuity and application the effect, after the first impact, declines to monotony and fatigue. For all its bravura and erotic postures, erotic writing is emotionally anaemic. Cleland may have understood or sensed this crucial deficiency in the medium for he recalls the tonic concept of love at the end of the book in the form of Charles, returned from his enforced voyage to the West Indies. Fanny's transports when she is reunited in bed with her lover are a fair example of Cleland's gentler rallies.

Writing in a debtor's prison, Cleland assembled a concentration of the kind of incidents which could and did happen episodically in his own time. There is almost no fantasy in the sense that we will see it developing later. But one little private day-dream of his own he indulged. When Charles returned to England, home, and Fanny, he was almost as poor as she had been when she first arrived in London—in much the same condition as the author, except that Charles was still at liberty but she in the meantime had been, in the course of her adventures, married and widowed by a rich old gentleman, and thus was now a woman of property who could painlessly dispel all her new husband's anxieties. Fanny did something of the same for her creator in real life; she changed his life and turned him into a man who could afford to be respectable, much as he had done to her at the end of the story, when, an honest but no less confiding woman, she says

> I could not help pitying, even in point of taste, those who, immersed in gross sensuality, are insensible to the so delicate charms of VIRTUE, than which even PLEASURE has not a greater friend, nor VICE a greater enemy.

With *The Memoirs of Fanny Hill*, the English Erotic novel had arrived. It was translated into almost every foreign language but there was nothing comparable to follow it at once. There was witty salaciousness like *The Delights of Venus*, and of course, aggressive bawdiness like *The Amorous Friars* (1760). Cleland, it should be remembered, never used a bawdy word. There were also picaresque adventures about pretty waifs in low life, like the *History of the Human Heart* (1769), and also, very significantly, a growth of works on the ancient and esoteric sport of flagellation, a subject which must be treated separately.

Towards the end of the century signs of a new disassociation from the processes of real life began to appear in erotic writing. *Fanny Hill*, while it reflected a perennial daydream of masculine immaturity which has been memorably fixed by Mr Larabee, as that 'somewhere, for someone, sex can be a full-time activity',[1] contained nothing improbable or removed from the experience of actual life, except for the overwhelming concentration of these episodes. An exotic never-neverland of vicarious sex began to bloom in surroundings which corresponded to nothing in the real life of the times. By 1824 *The Voluptarian Cabinet* ushers us into the lush extravagences of Gothic fancy, a palatial establishment for the recreation of rich and aristocratic ladies.

> I have purchased very extensive premises which are situated between two great thoroughfares, and are entered from each by means of shops devoted entirely to such trades as are exclusively resorted to by ladies.

[1] Larrabee: *The Cultural Content of Sex Censorship*, 20 Law and Contemp. Prob. 672, 683–684 (1955).

In the areas between two rows of houses I have erected a most elegan temple, in the centre of which are large saloons entirely surrounded with boudoirs most elegantly and commodiously fitted up. In these saloons according to their classes are to be seen the finest men of their species I can procure, occupied in whatever amusements are adapted to their taste, and all kept in a high state of excitement by good living and idleness.

The ladies will never enter the saloons even in their masks, but view the inmates from a darkened window in each boudoir. In one they will see fine elegantly dressed young men playing at cards, music etc.—in others athletic men wrestling, or bathing in a state of perfect nudity—in short you will see such a variety of the animal that they cannot fail of suiting their inclinations. Having fixed upon the one she would like to enjoy the lady has only to ring for the chambermaid, call her to the window, point out the object and he is immediately brought to the boudoir. She can enjoy him in the dark, or have a light and keep on her mask; she can stay an hour or a night, and have one or a dozen men as she pleases, without being known to any of them . . . and to elevate the mind to the sublimest raptures of love, every boudoir is surrounded with the most superb painting of Aretino's Postures after Julio Romano and Ludoviccion Carracci, interspersed with large mirrors: also a side board covered with the most delicious viands and richest wines. The whole expense of the institution is defrayed by a subscription from each lady of one hundred guineas per annum, with the exception of the refreshments, which have to be paid for at the time.

We have looked at a number of cases of writing which at some time or other has been deemed obscene, in the meaning of offensively shocking or disgusting, and we have seen the subsequent emergence from independent stock of writing which has been held to be obscene in the meaning of 'verbal aphrodisiac', alluring to libidinous thoughts. Literature, as I have tried to show, cannot in its cathartic nature be obscene, and art can be as well distilled from commonplace as from exceptional lives, from the criminal as from the law-abiding, from obscenity as from propriety. The achievements of Jane Austen and Marcel Proust cannot be measured by the human material they used. Time usually makes a fool of the censor and it is too easy to illustrate these arguments with references to classics of English literature— Thomas Hardy, obscene in 1895, great writer by 1925; James Joyce 'infamously obscene' in 1923, ennobled in 1933—but the question may very fairly be asked, What of the failures, works produced by writers perhaps capable of literature, which in these instances do not rise to those heights, and weighed down by the unsublimated obscenity of their content, rest predominantly *obscene*: do they *remain* obscene? In practice the problem seldom arises because the test of time relegates those failing in universality to extinction or to an obscurity which only unshockable bibliophiles will disturb. The odd freak cases like *The Well of Loneliness*, where curiosity value somewhat outlives merit, may be found to have had the charge of obscenity lifted from them, not because of their redeeming literary virtue, but because of changing standards of obscenity. There are however a few very interesting cases yet untested by exposure, of which perhaps the outstanding are a pair of poems 'Don Leon' and 'Arabella' by Lord Byron.[1] Here I find myself faced with the very problem with which these essays are concerned: how much to show? and now I plainly lay myself open to the taunt, 'Libertarian, free thyself.' I am perfectly ready to justify the publication of these poems in their entirety, but in writing anything one must bear in mind the appropriateness as a matter of taste and context of what is written.

I suppose that as well as readers interested in literature and the question of freedom in written communication, the familiar prurient prude may get this book into his hands in a zealous quest for the pleasure of being shocked. I would not deny him his pleasure, but what follows is addressed to the reader of this book as a whole.

The subject matter of 'Leon' and its sister poem, 'Arabella', was when the verse was written and is still today, grossly obscene in the view of the majority of people, and I am putting my contention to the severest test when I claim them for literature. I say that they are not obscene. There are two central themes: an examination of the nature of and an apologia for paederasty, and an account of the circumstances leading to the commission by Byron upon his wife of the practice, usually associated with paederasty, which, it was alleged, was a cause of Lady Byron's estrangement from her husband. Now these were themes which undoubtedly would have shocked John Cleland; indeed of one he expressed his horror through the mouth of Fanny, and the other he did not permit to be realised, though it was once attempted. Yet John Cleland's book, well written as it was for that class of book, is obscene within the meaning of our terms, and calculated to provoke libidinous thoughts, while, in my submission, 'Don Leon' is not obscene in any sense. The demands made by the poem simultaneously at several levels of thought and sensibility

---

[1] *An Epistle from Lord Byron to Lady Byron* explaining the real cause of the external separation. It was described as 'having been found' in a cottage by the roadside about a mile from the Porta all'orgine near Pisa.—Ed.

upon the reader are such that the contemplation of obscenity is not itself obscene, to those capable of appreciating the verse; to other readers, if any, the poem might prove too obscure either to corrupt or to educate. The poems are not in fact by Byron, at least not in their entirety, and in the opinion of most of Byron's modern biographers, not at all by him. This conclusion has been reached by internal evidence, allusions to incidents such as the Banks prosecution, which Byron could not have known of. Yet the verse is so vigorously and consistently, and sometimes so excellently Byronic, that it is difficult to banish the suspicion that some parts of it may have been composed by the author of 'Don Juan'. Whose skilled hand, if not Byron's, it was that composed them and the rest of the work in so confident a cast of the poet's style and sustained articulation, is not known.

The verse glides easily, Byronically, from rhetoric to tender reverie, and from cynical irony to satirical scorn. There is no overlay of bawdy words, nor any contrived introduction of carnal activity which does not have intrinsic and undeniable life in a body of feeling inseparably engaged to thought.

He recalls a pubescent girlish playfellow and his own shy inexperience

> There on the grass as we recumbent lay,
> Not coy wast thou, nor I averse to play
> And in that hour, thy virtue's sole defence
> Was not thy coldness, but my innocence.

The seeds of the ambivalence in his nature began to stir at school when things went wrong

> Flying for solace to a comrade's breast.
> In lonely walks their vows of friendship pass,
> Warm as the shepherd to his rustic lass.
> Their friendship ripens into closer ties
> They love. Then mutual vague desires arise.

Later self-consciousness grows.

> Full well I know though decency forbad
> The same caresses to a rustic lad;
> Love, love it was that made my eye delight
> To have his person ever in my sight.

Then he regards the consequential clouds that gather over the head
of him assailed with

> . . . secret longings to pursue
> Those inspirations which if books speak true
> Have led e'en priest and sages to embrace
> Those charms which female blandishments efface.

The feeling here is flawed with that moral vulgarity to which
paederasts and other persecuted companies are prone, a tendency to
exalt their practices to the status of a mystical sacrament, and to view
themselves as pleiades of esoteric superiority.

However noble the character of our paederast in all other respects,
though he devote his life and fortune to the reform of cruel injustice,
yet

> Let but some knave vituperate his name
> Adieu to all his former well earned fame!
> An exile to a foreign land he'll fly
> Neglected live and broken-hearted die.

The argument is steady enough here, but there is a querulous note
in the tone; for a moment thought and feeling part company. Unity
returns in one of the most notable passages in the poem:

> I love a youth, but Horace did the same;
> If he's absolved say why am I to blame?
> When young Alexis claimed a Virgil's sighs,
> He told the world his choice and may not I?
> Shall every schoolman's pen his verse extol,
> And, sin in me, in his a weakness call?
> Then why was Socrates surnamed the sage,
> Not only in his own, but every age,
> If lips, whose accents strewed the path of truth,
> Could print their kisses on some favoured youth?
> Or why should Plato in his Commonwealth,
> Score tenets up which I must note by stealth?
> Say, why, when great Xpaminondas died,
> Was Cephidorus buried by his side?
> Or why should Plutarch with eulogiums cite
> That chieftain's love for his young catamite,
> And we be forced his doctrines to decry,
> Or drink the bitter pill of infamy?

The storm clouds open and, amidst peals of thunder, a martyr's crown is vouchsafed.

> Oh! England with thy hypocrite's cant,
> To hear the bench declaim, the pulpit rant,
> Who would not say that chastity's pure gems
> Had shed their lustre o'er the muddy Thames?
> That self-condemned, decreed ineffable,
> Innominate, this blackest sin of hell,
> Had fled dismayed to some Transalpine shore
> To sully Albion's pudic cliffs no more?
> Marked you the thousand inkhorns that indite
> With ruthless glee the name of some poor wight
> By Bow Street bloodhounds to their Jeffreys brought,
> With flap unbuttoned in some tap-room caught?

The themes in both poems overlap in parts and are repeated with variations. Some of what Don Leon is made to say is in the form of an address to his wife on the supposed cause of their estrangement.

> What lot was mine—and, on my wedding night,
> What viands waited for my appetite—
> I will not say: but e'en the best repast,
> Repeated often surfeits us at last.
> The surfeit came: to this my crime amounts,
> I fain would slake my thirst from other founts.
> But, not like those, who with adultrous steps
> Seek courtesans and hackney'd demireps,
> I left thee not beneath a widow's quilt,
> To take another partner of my guilt.
> Thy charms were still my refuge—only this
> I hope to find variety in bliss.

At other times the poet addresses the reader directly in his account of what converse passed between Byron and his wife in their marriage bed.

> She bad me speak of wonders I had seen,
> In cities where my wandering steps had been
> 'Tell me,' she said, 'Of strange and jealous men
> In secret Harems whome their consorts pen,
> Of bluebeard Turks on Ottomans reclined,
> And young sultanas to their wills resigned.'

Leon discourses obligingly of exotic sights and adventures, but
inexorably his mind is drawn back to contemplation of his favourite
visions of delight and, in the circumstances, one may think, with somewhat improbable naïvety the lady breaks the flow:

> 'Dear Leon,' interrupting here my tale,
> My wife exclaimed, 'Can male then covet male?
> Can man with man hold intercourse of love
> And mar the ends designed by God above?'

He then acquaints her with certain supplementary facts of life, and
in the process provokes in himself desire for a forbidden mutation and

> O, lovely woman by your maker's hand
> For man's delight and solace wisely planned,
> Thankless is she who nature's bounty mocks
> Nor gives love entrance where he knocks.

Then he advances part sardonic, part compassionate, part almost
romantic, no part erotic, shirking nothing, to the indulgence which
was to be the cause—through his wife's subsequent remorse and confession to her mother, and that lady's fervent espousal of the opportunity offered for a dramatic grievance—of the ugly rupture of his
marriage and the unextinguishable scandal it fired.

> An other path untrodden yet remains,
> Where pleasure in her close recesses reigns,
> The neophyte to that more hallowed spot
> But rarely ventures 'tis the favourite grot
> Where sages, prelates, kings and bards retire
> To quench the rage of Priapeian fire.
> How many view this grotto from afar,
> Whilst fear and prejudice, the entrance bar!
> There fain the pedagogue's lewd glance would reach
> Through the convulsions of a schoolboy's breech.
> There as the youth with tightened pantaloons,
> Whirls though the dance in waltz or rigadoons,
> Or Misses' haunches wriggle in quadrilles
> In thought the lecher his libation spills.
> . . . .
> Then turn thee round, indulge a husband's wish,
> And taste with me this truly classic dish.

'Don Leon' and 'Anabella' were an unrepeatable curiosity. It was
the last occasion for many generations that rabid obscenity could be

disarmed and transmuted into literature. One step forward takes us into
the Victorian age and obscenity, or anything that could be so interpreted by the most eager imagination is banished from literature and
a formula for the worst of both worlds is achieved. Literature is
emasculated, and obscenity repudiated as an element of reality to be
understood and sublimated, is driven underground, where, instead of
wasting away, it waxes fat and proliferates into a teeming tribe of
calibans. Pornography was the secret price that Victorian propriety
had to pay to purchase its public image: blackmail paid to the Id to
keep out of sight. The strain of what was going on under those top
hats and behind those severe and frowning side-whiskered faces finds
utterance in the joyless, revengeful nature of obscene periodicals like
The Cremorne; and it was pillars of society—like J. Campbell,[1] who
produced the *Amatory Experiences of a Surgeon*—who *wrote* as well as
read this melancholy stuff. A striking characteristic of this class of
work is the degradation of sex from an operation of healthy delight
to one of gloating, ritual, self-conscious defilement. The minds at
which this writing is aimed had already lost, or had never developed,
the capacity for enjoying sexual relations of any kind, their substitute
and their form of 'pleasure' was the desecration of that which they
were themselves incapable of enjoying. 'Dirty', as a term applied to
sexual matters, is usually just a subjective and irrational expression of
hostility. When both the writer and any reader who enjoys it must
feel it to be so, when the whole purpose of the communication is to
provoke a feeling of dirtiness, when all the characters in the action
feel, and *show* that they feel, dirty about what they are doing and that
if they did not feel dirty it would not be worth doing, the word takes
on an objectively applicable meaning.

The psychological distortions produced by the prolonged sustain-
ment of acutely false public posture were near intolerable; some relief
was obtained by those outbursts of rage which so frequently figure
in the illustrations and anecdotes of the Victorian male, some relief
in brief clandestine transactions, and some, we see, from the enormous
output from the books which were in a locked case in the study. The
introduction to a Victorian pornographic magazine[2] is revealing:

> Having decided to bring out a journal the editor racks his brains for a
> suitable name with which to christen his periodical. Friends are usually useless
> in emergencies of this kind, but at last our own ideas have hit upon the modest
> little 'Pearl' as more suitable, especially in the hope that, when it comes under

---

[1] A pseudonym. His real name was J. C. Reddie.   [2] *The Pearl.*

the snouts of the moral and hypocritical swine of the world they may not
trample it underfoot and feel disposed to rend the publisher and that a few
will become subscribers on the quiet. To such better disposed piggywiggies
I would say for encouragement that they only have to keep up appearances
by regularly attending church, giving to charities and always appearing
deeply interested in moral philosophy to ensure a respectable and highly
moral character, and that if they only are clever enough *never to be found out*,
they may *sub rosa* study and enjoy the philosophy of life till the end of their
days, and earn a glorious and saintly epitaph on their tombstones when at
last the devil lays them to rest.

The infantile coprology, wholly unattractive and repellent to the
great majority of us today, was a large part, but only part, of Victorian pornography. Some of it was quite cheerful, even romantic in
tone, and at least aimed at inspiring some feeling of gaiety rather than
defilement. One of the better erotic magazines was *The Pearl*, part of
the introduction to which is quoted above. But O, what a fall is here
from 'Don Leon', *Fanny Hill*, even from the sub-mandarinese of *The
Volptarian Cabinet*. The old disciplines of style had disintegrated in the
flood of popular education without having been replaced; the writing
is clumsy and weak, the tone frivolous or maudlin, we have entered
the first phase of the world of the modern fiction magazine. There
are two main classes of story: the 'swaggering hilarious' which opens
with the conventional clatter and attack of a juvenile adventure
tale:

> Fast friends! I should rather think Captain Bob Slap and Dick Dash were
> fast friends; both were of the Foot Guards and they were so fast that they had
> out run the constable, given their creditors the go-bye and were going at a
> devil of a pace to the dogs.

Then there is the adventure 'sensual and sentimental', a fantasy
which is usually placed in the security of idyllic palatial or pastoral
setting.

> My uncle's is a nice country residence standing in large grounds of its own
> and surrounded by small fields of arable and pasture land, interspersed by
> numerous interesting copses, through which run foot-paths and shady
> walks where you are not likely to meet anyone in a month.[1]

The writer purports to be a youth describing an extremely eventful
stay with his cousins at his uncle's country house. There are Frank

[1] *Sub-Umbra, or Sport Among the She Noodles* (*The Pearl*).

and his two sisters of which Walter's sights are first set at eighteen year old Annie,

> a finely developed blonde with deep blue eyes, pouting red lips and a full heaving bosom which to me looked like a perfect volcano of smothered desires.

Frank was too lazy to go for a walk, so

> 'Come on Annie,' said I, taking her hand; 'Frank is in love.'
> 'No, I am sure he never thinks of girls except his sisters,' was the reply. We were now out of earshot in a shady walk so I went on a little more freely. 'But, surely you, coz, are in love, if he is not; I can tell it by your liquid eye and heaving bosom.' A scarlet flash shot over her features at my allusion to her finely moulded (sic), but it was evidently pleasing to her and far from offensive to judge from her playfully spoken 'Oh Walter, for shame, sir!'

The story runs on in this vein for some time, much the same in essential character as modern romantic short-story magazines quite openly on sale today in England and America. Walter kisses her 'ruby lips' and taxes her with knowledge of 'love', challenging her to say it is a 'stranger' to her bosom. She continues to blush obligingly and when he kisses her again, 'rapturously' this time, she fairly 'trembles' with emotion.

> She seemed on fire, a thrill of emotion seemed to shoot through both of us, and for several moments she lay almost motionless in my arms, with one hand resting on my thigh . . .

Full of hope Walter is about to proceed

> but she suddenly roused herself, saying 'We must never stop here, let us walk round or they will suspect something.'

Thwarted of Annie, Walter consoles himself that night with Frank. Here must be noted the sexual versatility of many of these vigorous Victorian youths and men; when not assailing the 'ruby lips' of blushing girls, they are quite liable to jump into each other's arms. This common ambivalence is all the more remarkable since there is very little purely homosexual writing at this time[1] although we know that

---

[1] In 1880 there was *The Sins of the Cities of the Plain, or the Recollections of a Mary Ann*. London, Leicester Square, and in 1883 *Letters from Laura to Evaline*; then in 1893 came *Teleny, or the Reverse of the Medal*, which was published as *Cosmopolis*, a turgid melodramatic homosexual novel in which Oscar Wilde may have had a hand. See C. R. Dawes. *Erotic Literature in England*, p. 252.

there was no lack of homosexual practice. I am at a loss to account adequately for this omission. One possibility which has occurred to me is that, while a homosexual harbouring a book containing descriptions of both homosexual and heterosexual practices would have an alibi, the social consequences of being found in possession of a book catering exclusively for homosexual tastes would have been so final and irremediable that it was a risk not many were prepared to take. Against this I must admit that I have seldom seen rational argument, however strong, prevail over compulsive psychological demands. However I offer this explanation, for what it is worth, as a hypothesis until a better supersedes it.

To return to Walter and Annie: next morning he renews the attack, taking her—it being 'gloriously warm and fine'—for another ramble. He gradually works the conversation round till it gets 'exceedingly warm' and he has Annie's cheeks colouring prettily again.

'What a rude boy you have grown, Walter, since you were here last, I can't help blushing at the way you run on, sir,' she exclaimed at last.

In Walter's excited reply we hear how low the Victorian male's boiling point was.

'Annie, my darling,' I replied, 'What can be more pleasant than to talk fun with pretty girls, the beauties of their legs and bosoms and all about them. How I should love to see your lovely calf at this moment, especially after the glimpse I have already had of a divine ankle.'

Walter is really warming up now and he throws himself under a 'shady tree' drawing the 'half-resisting girl' down on the grass at his side, and kissing her passionately, murmurs

'Oh, Annie, what is there worth living for but the sweets of love?'

Walter means business and there is a great deal about 'darts of love' and 'mossy grottos'; her lips meet his in a 'fiery embrace', but just when he seems to be making some headway

suddenly disengaging herself, her eyes cast down and looking awfully abashed, she stammered out, 'What is it, what do you mean, Walter?'

Walter manages to retain his self-control and, with remarkable patience, begins lesson one all over again, but after several unsuccessful attempts to communicate to her what is in his mind, he is constrained to exclaim, '. . . Is it possible you do not know what it is for?'

At last perseverance is rewarded and he sees his goal in sight, not forgetting to take certain discreet precautions:

> ... for fear of damaging her dress or getting the green stamp of the grass on the knees of my light trousers I persuaded her to stand up by the gate ...

Annie stands and modestly hides her face in her hands on the top rail of the meadow gate and Walter takes stock of 'glories unfolded to view' the mere mention of which must have sharply raised the erotic temperature of the Victorian reader.

> ... her lovely legs, drawers and stockings making a *tout ensemble*.

But alas, it is not Walter's day. He stands and is about to take possession of his prize when

> ... a sudden shriek from Annie, her clothes dropped, all my arrangements were upset in a moment; a bull had unexpectedly appeared on the opposite side of the gate and frightened my love by the sudden appearance of his cold damp nose on her forehead. It is too much to contemplate the scene even now.

There, as far as I can communicate an impression of it in brief, is the epitome of the benign Victorian erotica, as opposed to the coprolitic obscenity to which I have referred earlier. I need to quote no more. *Sub-Umbra, or Sport Among the She Noodles* is the beginning and end of it, and all the others, *Lady Pockinham, or They All Do It* and the rest, differ significantly only in the interesting incidental revelations of social history they yield as a by-product. The essentials of the fantasy are always the same: young men of superhuman vigour; at first shy and resisting, but later compliant, tender and passionate girls; unlimited and repeated opportunities. It served its purpose and may have been of some real benefit to generations that needed it. The vehemence of the exclamations in these underground vicarious celebrations are sometimes pathetically yearning.

> Such were my amours then. I was barely twenty years old. My heart still rejoices at these simple pleasures and this happy day. O Truth, O Nature!

In this class were books like *Venus in India* which enjoyed the additional advantage of an exotic setting, which generally have a formal almost prim introduction:

> I must crave your pardon and beg you to permit me the use of my pen, else I shall feel it difficult to describe, as I hope to, the full joys I so happily revelled in during the five happy years I spent in Hindustan.

But the great mass of Victorian pornography was not like *The Pearl*, and had the self-consciously ugly and crippled relationship to sex. We must remember that sexual tensions and the impulse to obscenity they inevitably generate had no healing outlet whatever in literature and the arts. Almost no honest feeling could be represented openly; the majority of underground outlets produced stuff like *The New Ladies' Tickler* in which characters seem to be in competition to introduce the largest number of four-, five-, and more letter obscenities in the course of sexual excitement. To a generation accustomed to being allowed to regard sex as one important and legitimate part of a larger whole, to looking at it with interest and without shame along with the other elements of life, and to seeing life on the whole freely examined through the arts, such furtive, scrabbling, panting obscenity is well-nigh incomprehensible. Readers of lewd trash like *The New Ladies' Tickler* were educated men, inevitably displaying a public front of assiduous propriety.

In *The Simple Tale of Susan Asked* the following dialogue takes place between Susan and her friend Lucia:

'Have you never read any novels or any love stories, Susan?' Lucia asked.

'No, my father and mother said they were poor foolish stuff.'

'I have heard them say so, and have you not even Sir Walter Scott or Shakespeare in the house?'

'Shakespeare we have, I know; but it is locked up in Papa's study in the glass book-case. I have never read it.'

'Ah, then read *Romeo and Juliet*, you may perhaps learn a secret or two.'

At the same time as girls were talking like that, their brothers might be furtively reading, or even writing, works like *Harlequin*, or rather probably something inferior, for *Harlequin, or Prince Cherrytop* was a curiosity above and apart from the normal low run of Victorian obscene *facetiae*. It was written by a group of young Oxford graduates and army officers, including, it has been said, George Augustus Sala. It takes the form of a pantomime and is in style just like any other contemporary pantomime performed in the London theatres, except that the quality of the verse and lyrics is much higher than is usual in that hackneyed medium. All the conventional ingredients are there, a fairy-tale court, a prince and princess, a curse, good and evil spirits, etc. There is, however, one unconventional element to the pantomime, and that is its theme. The action begins as pantomimes in the 1870's always did with the dark scene, showing the forces of evil that are menacing the hero. The venue is the cavern of the Demon Mastur-bation who has laid a curse upon Prince Cherrytop the heir to the throne making him a martyr to onanism. And this is not all; part of the curse is that everyone in his presence must do as he does.

The obscenity is adolescent, offensive and gross, but perfectly harmless. It is schoolboy dirty jokes reinforced with adult wit, for although many people may understandably find it disgusting, it is still at moments hilarious to anybody who can still laugh at Rabelais and Chaucer.

But it simply could not happen today, the conspiracy of an 'ob-scenity resistance movement' uniting men of superior education and talents, and no doubt of superior responsibilities in a planned campaign to write, as it were, forbidden sex-burlesque words on walls.

Apart from the aggressively ugly coprolitic revenge motive, there are two clearly identifiable impulses in Victorian underground writing: the bitter and the sweet.

This division sounds a rather contrived simplification but in fact this clear-cutness is very much part of the Victorian attitude. It can be found in the blacks and whites of Dickens, in Jekyll and Hyde, in Dorian Grey and his portrait.

Here is the sweet; in one of the better written works of Victorian erotica, and the one above most others that bears the mark of authentic personal experience, blended with anecdote and fantasy, is called *The Memoirs of a Voluptuary*. A tight comradeship of boys, English and French, at an English boarding school embark on a most complex and well-told series of erotic adventures, bearing them in all directions, including to Paris. In the end the consortium is broken because one of their number must go to Sandhurst Military College. In an epilogue, the author, looking back, says

> I could not congratulate myself sufficiently on having the good fortune to make such staunch friends; both work and play were so congenial that I was as happy as the day is long. There could not be four better comrades than myself and my three special chums, and I do not think we ever had a serious dispute or difference during the whole time we were associated together. I often now go over the fun we had and, if it were possible to fulfil such a wish, I would be glad to live through this period once more. There is a freshness and vivacity about boyhood that never comes a second time, once it is past, but fortunately memory remains, and carries the recollection with us to brighten our after years. Charles Lamb says in his Essays of Elia that it is not

good or advisable for grown people to associate intimately with the young; but I for one refuse to bow to the weight of his authority. I have always found the greatest delight in juvenile society, speaking as a man, and I can regard with some envy those fortunately placed persons, such as schoolmasters, who pass their lives in the midst of a perennial atmosphere of youth and are able themselves to retain a youthfulness of spirit even in advancing age. But I must not stop thus to moralise . . .

Nor did he.

And the bitter: it suddenly appears cold and repulsive as a corpse at a feast in the midst of priapic merrymaking. Who would guess that the following passage, which I will quote in full, the observations of a widely experienced woman of the world, came from a work of erotic pornography:

> I think that I have already demonstrated that I am a hypocrite. Society obliges everyone to be a hypocrite. The difference is only in degrees, the necessity is universal. . . . Is not ever evasion of the truth a smooth, plausible hypocrisy? Nobody believes it all the same; that is the strangest part of it. It is offered and accepted. Everybody excuses it, weighs it at its own fictitious value and passes it on. 'Tell the truth and shame the Devil'—that shabby proverb goes a certain way. I almost think after a certain study of the subject that Society would be more ashamed, in spite of its usual disregard of that sentiment, *if it had to tell the truth*. A just sense of the value of hypocrisy, of its judicious use, its employment, is absolutely necessary if you would shine in the flickering light of Society. Yet I am not afraid of criticism. I defy criticism to do me harm. It would certainly not do me any good . . . I meet in every saloon, in every boudoir the saintly Cannon who cannot keep his fingers off his choristers, the elderly lordling who apes the vices of a Domitian or a Nero; the minister of religion who ministers to the lambs of his flock in more senses than one; and the more blatant pretentious man about town who divides his attentions between his exaggerated shirt collar and his simpering partner. He would delight to be the very devil himself if only he knew how! There too are the lonely, loving hearts, who in that never resting vortex, watch long and sadly for the coming of one they dreamed of in days now gone, or who mourn unceasingly the one who will never return—whose hope never flags, whose faith is intact beneath the false mask they must wear—who will be as content as I shall be to give it all—to submit to the inevitable when it comes.

Pornography, then, could sometimes provide an outlet for some unlikely and unpornographic states of mind, which might not have reason to exist today, or if they did exist could be adequately expressed and communicated in life and literature. But extension of freedom offers a means, not a ready-made panacea, and we must remember that while we have been released from strains which the Victorians had to bear, we have also attracted to us psychological strains which they did not know, perhaps the most significant of which is a disillusionment with the fruits of egalitarianism and material prosperity, all of which inevitably expresses itself in the mutations of sexual ambitions, standards and relationships.

It is chastening to find that the most ubiquitous of Victorian deviations, flagellation, far from having gone out with aspidistras, has increased and multiplied and the demand for books in England and America today is larger than ever. The family tree of erotic flagellation may be traced back in the temple of *Artemis*, to the altars of *Dionysos-Bacchus*, to the Etruscans *fufluns*, but these were not its beginnings. The appeal of the cult is as persistent as it is ancient and it has maintained an unbroken cabal of secret associations through successive centuries. It was lively in the eighteenth century—Cleland has a flagellation scene in *Fanny Hill*, but only one, and clearly Cleland, the most normal of sensualists was no enthusiast, but just wanted to be sure he had left out no contemporary practice. But in the nineteenth century it broke out in a conflagration of sympathetic and contagious fervour. It is rare to find a Victorian erotic book without some element of flagellation, and many works are wholly or almost wholly designed to cater to this taste: *Frank and I, Secrets of Women, The Birchen Bouquet, The Mysteries of Verbena House, Dolly Morton* (America's most notable contribution), *Country Retirement, Miss Coote's, Confessions, The Convent School* . . . the list could be extended indefinitely. The practices were heterosexual, homosexual, active, passive or both. The members of the flagellation cabal tended to be the pharisees of pornography; indeed they would probably have been indignant to have the description pornographic applied to their esoteric donations; nevertheless, within the meaning of our terms, that is what they were; they were written to provoke libidinous thoughts in those susceptible. The flagellant was forever giving thanks that he was not as other men. One rather superior entertainment begins

> In the following pages will be found no vulgar words, no blasphemies, no sneers at sacred things. We have but depicted with too graphic a pen the accidents of a practice in itself commendable, nay, enjoined. What need to quote King Solomon and Dr Johnson, sages both
>
> *Quae narrare nefas lex tamen esse sinit.*

The author of 'Don Leon' had words for them, especially for the ordained pedagogics:

> Flog you lechers, flog, each measured stroke adjust
> 'Tis well your cassock hides your rising lust.

The subject of flagellation produced on the whole the best writing in the files of Victorian 'obscenity', it seemed to inspire its votaries with a peculiar creative zeal, and among their number were distinguished men of letters and one of the major poets of the century.

The paederastic flagellation stories and poems lovingly written and read by Swinburne were usually set in schools, and in the racy gusto of their tone and style were perfect models of 'wholesome' English school stories.

> 'Who's to be swished, Charlie?' said Harry Fane: 'Well,' said Charlie, 'I am for one, hang it, and your major is, Anstruther, and Phil Acton and Percy Fielding, and both Seytons, and Reggie Shirley, and I think Fred and Hugh and Tom Ainslie, and Ned Wyatt and Willie Goring, and Chavering— not the old one, Arthur—and Harry Redfern.'
> 'I'm jolly glad he's in too,' said Earnie, 'Beast of a bully, he is.'[1]

It was to be a field day. The story proceeds with a vivid description of the flogging of Reggie Fane, told with the breathless concentration and attention to detail of enthusiastic spectators of an athletic contest.

The underlying paederastic eroticism of the Victorian heroic sado-masochist makes itself felt immediately in the favourite mixture of menace and caress with which an appetising 'virgin' victim is tenderly described.

> Aubrey Wilton, just twelve, had been two months at school and not had a flogging, a thing unheard of at Birchminster. He was the prettiest boy there, with perfectly straight pure features, pale roses in the cheeks, thick brown eyebrows and eyelashes, light brown curls that were golden and tawny or darker and warmer as sun and shade was on them, great wild eyes like a wild animal's, and unluckily a skin too white and tender for a girl. He was a quick healthy boy, fresh and brave in his way, but never inured to pain or punishment; spoilt by his mother, brothers, tutor and schoolfellows; a nice boy enough by nature, and so handsome in mould of form and type of face that his beauty won upon all, and his natural grace of manner drew them close towards him. Older boys did his verses, kept off bullies, excused him fagging, yet his own division did not hate or spite him. He was quick enough with a little help not to come to grief for some time, but his day was come now.

[1] From the *Whippingham Papers*.

When Swinburne celebrates in verse the gratification of his favourite taste he works himself up gradually with ritual invocations into a state of ecstatic self-hypnosis. I do not have to quote from the more abandoned and indecent verses to illustrate this quality.

> Oh, Birch whose mouth should sing of thee if not mine
> Is there a schoolboy oftener flogged than I am
> Have I not marks upon me still of thine?
> Is there a boy, I say, from here to Siam,
> Between the ages of eighteen and nine
> Or has there been a boy since the age of Priam
> In days unknown or in days unsearched
> Who has been oftener or more soundly birched.
>
> Right well thou knowest this voice that now invokes
> Thine oft experienced inspiration
> By all the rods I have felt and all the strokes
> By all the burning pangs of my probation
> By all salt brine in which thy keeper soaks
> Thy twigs to make them fit for flagellation
> By their green buds that make one hate the spring
> By all their suppleness and all their sting.

And so on through fifty-two blood-stained verses describing in rich detail a massacre on the flogging block.

The taste for flagellation appears in many permutations, not always is it as severe and sanguinary as Swinburne's visions, but sometimes more so. With *The Pleasures of Cruelty* (1898), for example, we are in the fantasies of extreme pathological sadism. Sir Charles Dacre is not only a monster of cruelty but an insatiable killer; his image has been revived and repeated in the horror 'comics' of infamous repute. But others in contrast were gentle, subtle and insinuating. In *Grandma's Story* (from *The Romance of Chastisement*) the whole tone is one of oblique, sly, whimsical sensuality. The author, St George H. Stock, was a retired army officer, a cultured and urbane libertine for whom ordinary and direct erotic stimuli may have seemed insipid. But what he pleased to write might be taken by an innocent or uninformed reader for 'innocent' if eccentric writing, until the climactic flowering of the story when the gracefully, even cosily, contrived sensuality of his appetites shed their fig leaves. The scene is the drawing-room of a country house about 1860. Four female figures sit and recline on sofas and cushions round the fire. One is an old woman, the other three,

her grandchildren, of various adolescent ages; the eldest of the girls,
Jane, is speaking:

Did you hear about Georgy, Gan. Georgy, or Georgina Graham is a
sprightly young lady of thirteen now reclining on a rug at her Grand-
mother's feet and looking with a blank expression of face. Jane and Alice
are Georgie's sisters, her elders respectively by three and two years. With
all of them 'Gan' is a favourite, and deservedly so, she being still a child
at heart and much more companionable than her daughter Mrs Graham,
who is heard of, not seen. Mr Graham likewise is invisible, and is a fussy
fool . . .

Jane: Did you hear of the scrape that Georgy's in?
Gan: No, my dear; I thought something must be wrong and my pretty
    peach blossom looks scared. What is it?
Jane: Tell her yourself, Georgy.
Georgy: Wouldn't deprive you of the pleasure. Tell her you.
Jane: Wait till I put some coals on first—how the wind does howl—now
    we're snug. Georgy, you must know, was awful naughty.
Georgy: There you go! Whenever anything is wrong I am sure to get the
    blame.
Jane: Why you told me yourself, you called Papa a stupid old fool.
Georgy: He was so aggravating about the letter bag.
Jane: Well, anyway, he complained to Mama. She's driven off to Bryerly to
    fetch Miss Kyle and when they come back, which will be in about an
    hour's time, Georgy's to be whipped.

It is hardly necessary to say that all three are whipped, though not
before 'Gan' has regaled them with tales of corporal punishment at
her boarding school in Regency days.

The flagellants' appetites may be suggested in essence by two
flashes of quotation from the active and the passive positions.

'Oh, Miss Harrie,' screamed out the pretty sufferer, moving her limbs in
the most wanton manner . . .

'Fear and shame were both gone: it was as though I was surrendering my
person to the embraces of a man whom I so loved I would anticipate his
wildest desires.'

The rest is diminution. Modern pornography in England and
America is mainly poor stuff. It is a repetition of all the familiar Victorian situations in degraded contemporary colloquy. The kind of
people who might feel the need to *write* pornography in the nineteenth and early twentieth centuries no longer do so. It is unthinkable

today that a group of scholars should unite their skill to produce something like *Harlequin*; at least I hope it is. Obscenity has been restored to literature for treatment as a legitimate facet of reality. We owe much to the literary laundries of Joyce and Lawrence, and Edmund Wilson and Montherlant, and Durrell and Henry Miller, who have bit by bit and by different means, reasserted the principle that when human life and human feeling become at times worldly soiled, what they need to clean them is understanding, not darkness.

Pornography would wither in the open air; it thrives on secrecy and prohibition. In this respect censorship is the ally and promoter of pornography, and the pornographic state of mind. Censorship is a negative, insatiable, fear-driven compulsion, an historically inevitable phenomenon, but not necessarily a permanent one.

I have tried to bring some primitive order to the manifestations of obscenity in English writing outside literature, and to contain much in a small compass. But I should be dishonest if I ended without reference to a work which refuses to fit into any of my rough-hewn, elementary classifications. It is not literature; the writing is clumsy, commonplace and awkward; it is packed with obscenity, and yet it is not pornography either, any more than the last testimony of a condemned man could be pornographic, whatever it invoked. It is the exact opposite of erotic fantasy which is the stuff of pornography; it is a naked documentary of a man's sexual life told by a human being with an unflinching photographic memory, what psychologists call 'total recall'. The book is called *My Secret Life* and we do not know the name of the author, but we know something about him. He was prosperous, leisured, upper middle class, he was able to travel. He was no scholar or man of letters, and there is not a flicker of creative imagination in his flat, careful record, yet suddenly an observation of detail, a snatch of dialogue scathes the mind with its authenticity; and leaves the reader shuddering. No, it certainly isn't erotic. The author, though he poses as the author's executor, wrote the book in eleven volumes and had a few copies, between ten and twenty, printed at his own expense for £1100 in Amsterdam about 1880. I know of the existence of only one copy, to which I have access. There may perhaps be another or others, surviving. One copy was sold by auction at the Hotel Druont in Paris about 1923 for £120 at the current exchange rate.

But the book is unique as a case history and should be preserved if only for clinical study. Its rambling, formless progress covers enough raw material to build *Lolita, Memoirs of Hecate County, Quiet Days at Clichy* ten times over. It may be possible to suggest some of the qualities of this strange document with a passage describing the experience of the author one evening in Vauxhall Gardens, then a fashionable and popular place of amusement for all classes of Londoners and which shows the kind of thing that went on there then. On the evening in question he was going to watch the fireworks.

I passed a woman leading a little girl dressed like a ballet girl, and looked at the girl who seemed about ten years old, then at the woman who winked. I stopped, she came up and said 'Is she not a nice little girl?' 'Yes a nice little girl,' I replied. 'Would you like to see her undressed?' The little girl kept tugging the woman's hand and saying 'Oh, do come to the fireworks.' A bargain for three sovereigns was soon struck. She told me to go out of the gardens first, get a cab and stop a little way from the entrance. In three minutes the woman and child joined me. At about five minutes' drive from Vauxhall we stopped, walked a little way, turned down a street, and after telling me to wait two or three minutes, she opened the door of a respectable little house with a latch key, went in and closed the door. A minute afterwards she opened the door and treading lightly, as she told me, I found myself in a parlour, out of which led a bedroom, both well furnished. Enjoining me to speak in a low tone I sat down and contemplated the couple. The woman was stout, full sized, good looking, dark, certainly forty, and dressed like a well to do tradeswoman. The girl's head was but a few inches above my waist and she certainly wasn't more than ten years, but for such age as nice and fleshly as could be expected. I was impatient but noticed and remarked 'Why, you have gas!'—a rare thing in these homes. 'Beautiful, is it not?' said the woman.

This Victorian Humbert Humbert then enjoys the opportunities afforded with both girl and woman and

We talked afterwards. She was not the mother, nor the aunt, though the child called her so; the child was parentless; she had taken charge of her and prevented her going to the workhouse. She was in difficulties, she must live, the child would be sure to have it done to her some day, why not make a little money by her? Someone else would if she did not. So spoke the middle-aged woman.

He stayed the night and remained to breakfast.

We ate and drank, I paid liberally and went away. White trousers and black tail coat were the full evening dress at Vauxhall, but ludicrous in the day. I recollect feeling ashamed as I walked out in that dress in the sunshine. She would not fetch a cab as she was most anxious about noise. She gave me full instructions where to write and have the girl again. About a fortnight afterwards I made an appointment, but she did not keep it. I went to the house and asked for her; a woman opened the door. 'Do you know her?' she asked. 'Yes.' 'She is not here and I don't know where she has gone—perhaps you are as bad as she is,' and she slammed the door in my face.

The passages quoted above, even though I have omitted the description of carnal details, might shock and harrow a reader, but they are too nakedly true and melancholy to 'corrupt', to induce any feeling except perhaps one of austerity. In my use of the word 'omitted' in the previous sentence, I advert to what must have already been apparent to the reader: the censorship which I have imposed upon myself in the course of choosing the illustrations included in this essay. The relationship of means to ends in the process of verbal communication creates a moral responsibility which no writer should be prepared to surrender to standards other than his own. I have followed my own judgment of fitness in making a choice, having regard to all the circumstances attending this publication. But this is not to say that I think that what I have omitted should not have been written or ought to be suppressed. If it was written it had to be written, it had to come out, but the harm, if harm it be, was done before the words were written, and if we dislike its appearance we should look back to the conditions which generated it.

We have seen something of what censorship can do. It is not just the malpractice but the whole 'concept' of censorship which is malign, and which has been shown time and time again to be imperfectly safeguarded by the moderate intentions of those who admitted or enlarged it. Censorship has an inevitable attraction for the least enlightened and most intolerant and regressive elements in society, those who throughout history are forever trying to put not only themselves into uniforms, but everyone else too. It is for this reason that the issue of pornography is an important one; it has been used, as blasphemy once was, to justify censorship.

Having looked frankly at pornography under strong daylight, it appears to me to be more sad than bad, certainly less malevolent than the conspiracies of misrepresentation which are projected every day by newspapers.

Scientific research into the reactions of readers, especially younger readers, to books commonly deemed 'offensive' is at last being undertaken by the Kinsey Foundation at the University of Indiana, and what they ultimately will have to say may bring some surprises. However, taking account of the growing weight which is given, sometimes in courts of law, to the recommendations of psychologists, there is one final point to be made. I, for one, would not be willing to acquiesce in having the frontiers of freedom of communications fixed by an orthodoxy of psychologists, or by any related clan of the social sciences, which, given the opportunity and power, could become just as oppressive to the freedom of the mind as any other ascendant priesthood.